☆ American Girl®
CHARACTER ENCYCLOPEDIA

WRITTEN BY CARRIE ANTON
AND ERIN FALLIGANT

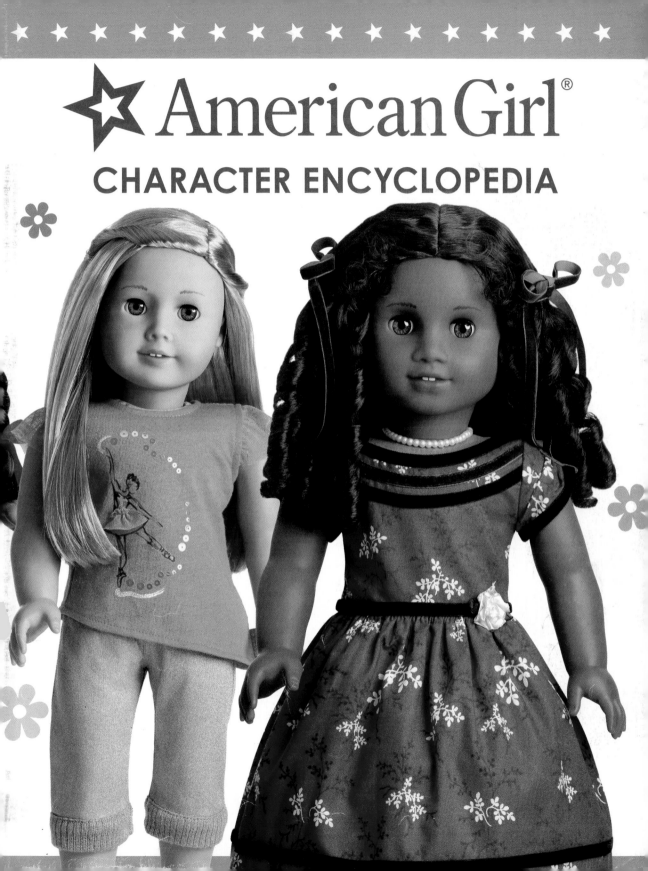

☆ American Girl®
CHARACTER ENCYCLOPEDIA

Contents

Chapter 1
American Girl® characters

From the BeForever™ characters of the past to the contemporary Girls of the Year™, these characters inspire today's girls to dream big and make a difference.

KAYA™

My year is 1764

Round hair ties

An adventurous girl, Kaya is a friend to the earth and animals. She dreams of becoming a courageous leader of her tribe, the Nez Perce. Kaya draws strength from her family, who help her prepare for whatever the future brings.

ALL ABOUT ME

★ Full name: **Kaya'aton'my'**

★ Name meaning: **She Who Arranges Rocks** (in Nez Perce)

★ Favorite activities: **Riding her horse, caring for animals, and swimming**

★ Favorite stories: **Grandmother's**

Furry friend

Kaya's dog, Tatlo, sticks by her side when she gathers food. Kaya places what she finds in a woven basket.

Moccasin booties

In This Year...

European settlers have not yet traveled as far as the Pacific Northwest, where the Nez Perce live.

Kaya's world

In the summer, Kaya and the Nez Perce people travel to find food, sleeping in tepees. In the winter, they live in permanent shelters called longhouses. The tribe celebrates its culture with singing, dancing, and feasts.

Tepee shelter

Pow-wow drum and mallet

Moveable shelter
Kaya's tepee is a cozy place to sleep. It is easy to pack up and carry when traveling with her tribe.

Winter wear
In the cold winter months, Kaya bundles up in layers of clothing, long mittens, and a furry hood.

Modern pow-wow outfit

FELICITY MERRIMAN™

My year is 1775

Felicity is growing up in colonial Williamsburg, Virginia, just before the start of the American Revolution, a war that sees America break away from British rule. Adventurous Felicity is never afraid to stand up for what she believes in.

Wide-brimmed straw hat

Floral embroidered gown

Gala gown

Even though she doesn't always enjoy dressing in ladylike clothes, Felicity is excited to go to the holiday ball. She wears a festive dress for the occasion.

ALL ABOUT ME

★ Nickname: **Lissie**

★ Favorite animal: **Horse**

★ Likes: **Horseback riding and playing with best friend Elizabeth**

★ Dislikes: **Embroidery, cooking, and dancing**

DID YOU KNOW?
Felicity learned to ride horses on her grandfather's plantation.

Felicity's world

For girls Felicity's age, "proper" pastimes include cooking, sewing, and dancing. But Felicity has an adventurous spirit and prefers exploring the outdoors while riding her horse, Penny.

Pattens

Fingerless mitts

Lacy pinner cap

Warm winter cloak

Winter warmers

In winter, Felicity keeps warm by putting on her mitts and slipping her hands inside an embroidered muff. She ties pattens to her shoes to keep her feet out of mud and puddles.

In This Year...

Many colonists, known as Patriots, want to break away from British rule. They begin planning how to gain independence.

In the stables

Felicity loves taking care of Penny's foal, Patriot. At night, she covers him with a cozy blanket to keep him warm.

ELIZABETH COLE™

Pierced ears

Coral pink taffeta gown

Born in England, Elizabeth is now growing up in Virginia. Her family are Loyalists, meaning that they want America to remain under British rule. Her best friend Felicity's family are Patriots who want America to become independent. Politics may divide Elizabeth and Felicity's families, but Elizabeth remains loyal to her good friend.

ALL ABOUT ME

★ Family nickname: **Bitsy**

★ Favorite lesson: **Sewing**

★ Secret wish: **To be as brave as Felicity**

★ Favorite pastime: **Poking fun at older sister Annabelle**

A proper young lady

Elizabeth and Felicity take classes to learn to dance, serve tea, and do fancy stitching and handwriting. They also learn how to curtsy to show respect when they meet someone important.

In This Year...

War is brewing. Patriots, unlike Loyalists, don't want to pay taxes to the king of England for things such as tea.

12

Elizabeth's world

For Elizabeth, life in Virginia feels very different from her old life in England. Teatime, however, feels the same, and with Felicity by her side, Elizabeth begins to feel at home.

Wooden tea caddy

Sugar bowl

Teatime gown

Time for tea

Elizabeth learns how to carefully measure the tea into the teapot. She then fills the teacups without spilling a drop!

DID YOU KNOW?
Elizabeth loves dancing! She dreams of attending a dance at the royal Governor's Palace.

Sleep tight

Elizabeth's home is large and elegant, but it can get chilly! She wears slippers to keep her toes toasty, and her four-poster bed has curtains to keep in warmth.

CAROLINE ABBOTT™

Bonnet

Brave Caroline dreams of being the captain of her own ship, like her father. Her spirit is tested when war comes to her hometown and she has to help rescue her father from the British enemy.

Sailing

Caroline's papa repairs a small sailboat that has been damaged in the war. He names the two-seater boat "Miss Caroline" and paints the name on the side.

Hem trimmed with tucks

In This Year...

The War of 1812 between the U.S. and Great Britain begins. The war lasts for three years, when both sides agree to make peace.

ALL ABOUT ME

★ Hometown: **Sackets Harbor, New York**

★ Favorite activities: **Sailing, fishing, and sewing**

★ Least favorite chore: **Baking**

★ Pet: **A black cat named Inkpot**

Caroline's world

Caroline's family runs a shipyard near Lake Ontario. Caroline loves being out on the water—whether it's sailing in the summer or ice-skating in the winter.

Braided hairpiece

On the lake
Caroline loves to glide along the frozen lake on her ice skates. Her blue coat with fur trim keeps her warm.

Brocade chair seats

Floral-detailed stripes

Happy birthday!
It's hard to get supplies during the war. For her birthday, Caroline is given a special treat of applesauce cake to enjoy around the table with her family.

DID YOU KNOW?
Caroline is an only child. She has no brothers or sisters.

JOSEFINA MONTOYA™

My year is 1824

Josefina lives on a New Mexican farm called a rancho. Ever since Mamá died, Josefina has tried to preserve her mother's traditions. But so much is changing! American traders arrive in New Mexico with new ideas. Josefina bravely faces these changes with hope.

Golden hoop earrings

Feast day

Instead of a birthday, Josefina celebrates the feast day of San José, the saint she was named after. She wears her mother's shawl and carries her lace fan.

ALL ABOUT ME

★ Favorite flower: **Primrose**
★ Pet: **A baby goat named Sombrita**
★ Best friend: **Mariana**
★ Activities: **Sewing, playing piano, and picking herbs and flowers**

Rebozo, or shawl

Soft moccasins with laces

DID YOU KNOW?

Josefina wants to be a healer. She makes a paste from a special plant to treat her friend's rattlesnake bite.

Josefina's world

Josefina spends most of her time at home on the rancho, helping to weave, garden, bake, and care for the animals. She also enjoys visiting the busy markets in Santa Fe.

Weaving
Josefina weaves on a Navajo Indian loom. She makes blankets and shawls for her family.

Straw hat with braided trim

Strap tightens under chin!

Ruffled calico riding dress

In This Year...

New Mexico is still part of Mexico, not the United States. But Americans visit Santa Fe to trade goods for the first time.

Fiesta!
Parties call for fancy clothing and delicious food. Josefina helps her family bake outdoors in an *horno*, or clay oven.

CÉCILE REY™

Velvet-trimmed hat with rosette

Cécile comes from a well-to-do family in New Orleans. She loves parties, but she makes time for helping others, too. Cécile enjoys volunteering at an orphanage, visiting the elderly, and teaching her friend Marie-Grace to speak French.

★ ALL ABOUT ME ★

★ Best friend: **Marie-Grace**

★ Favorite snack: **Pralines (sweet treats made with pecan nuts, cream, and sugar)**

★ Favorite hobbies: **Charades, reciting poems, and acting out plays**

★ Dreams for the future: **To be a stage actress and to travel the world**

In the parlor

Cécile sits at her desk to write letters to her older brother, Armand. He's been studying in Paris, France, for two years. She misses him very much.

In This Year...

There are many free people of color in New Orleans in 1853. They have more education and opportunities than black people anywhere else in the United States.

Cécile's world

Confident Cécile loves being in the spotlight. Whether it's putting on a pretend performance or dancing at a party, Cécile always shines.

Clever pet
Cécile finds that her parrot, Cochon, has a gift for speaking! He mimics her words, especially if she rewards him with pecan nuts.

Velvet hair ribbons

Desk with hidden seat

DID YOU KNOW?
Cécile sings off-key! She'd much rather act out plays or recite poetry than sing a song in front of an audience.

Posy print dress

Costume ball
In Cécile's time, balls for white people and black people are separated. She and Marie-Grace decide to wear the same masked costume so they can switch places and attend both balls.

MARIE-GRACE GARDNER ™

Shy Marie-Grace returns to New Orleans after four years away—but so much has changed! She worries that she will never make new friends and feel at home again.

DID YOU KNOW?
Marie-Grace has two nicknames. Her mother called her "Ti-Marie," and the children she visits at the orphanage call her "Marie-the-Great."

Golden heart-shaped locket

Fan for hot days

Summer nights
Hot New Orleans summers bring swarms of mosquitoes. At night, Marie-Grace sleeps beneath a mosquito net to protect herself from bug bites.

ALL ABOUT ME

★ Best friend: **Cécile Rey**
★ Best furry friend: **Argos, her shaggy dog**
★ Favorite activities: **Helping Papa at his doctor's office and exploring the French Market**
★ Special talents: **Singing, arithmetic, and entertaining children**

Marie-Grace's world

Marie-Grace's worries about fitting in are over when she meets Cécile. Her outgoing new friend helps Marie-Grace feel confident and inspires her to help others by volunteering at an orphanage.

Adjustable mirror

Fashionable ringlets

Getting ready

Marie-Grace washes up at her vanity stand and adds a splash of perfume—either lavender or rosewater. She's ready to volunteer at the orphanage.

Sateen jacket with ribbons

In This Year...

A yellow fever outbreak leads to many deaths in New Orleans and other parts of Louisiana. Yellow fever is carried by mosquitoes.

Striped skirt over pantalettes

Under the sun

Marie-Grace and Cécile have lots of fun together in the vibrant city of New Orleans. They use parasols to protect themselves from the bright sun.

KIRSTEN LARSON™

Gingham-check sun bonnet

When Kirsten moves to America from Sweden with her family, she feels like she will never belong in her new home. But Kirsten wants to be brave like her mother and she tries her hardest to make the best of her new life.

Home sweet home

Kirsten wears an embroidered apron from Sweden to bake Swedish treats. Celebrating her traditions makes her feel less homesick.

DID YOU KNOW?
Kirsten had a hard time fitting in at school at first, but she soon made friends.

Blue calico dress

ALL ABOUT ME

★ Born in: **Ryd, Sweden**

★ Lives in: **Minnesota Territory**

★ Favorite toy: **Sari, her rag doll**

★ Hobbies: **Exploring the outdoors, sewing, and baking**

Kirsten's world

In Minnesota, Kirsten and her family mix old traditions with new ones. One of Kirsten's favorite Swedish holiday traditions is Saint Lucia Day, celebrated on the darkest day of the year.

Floral-painted details

Saint Lucia wreath

Mix it up
Swedish and American treats combine to make an extra special Christmas feast in Kirsten's new home of Minnesota.

Woven table runner

In This Year...
Just like Kirsten and her family, many people move from Europe and the east coast of America to settle on the frontier.

Lace-trimmed Saint Lucia gown

Old and new
In her brand-new bed, Kirsten cuddles her old ragdoll that she brought with her from Sweden. Her new school friends made this colorful quilt just for Kirsten.

ADDY WALKER™

Addy is a courageous girl growing up during the Civil War. After she and her mother escape from slavery in the South to start a new life in Philadelphia, she dreams of reuniting with her father, brother, and baby sister. Addy always holds on to her hope for better days ahead.

Golden hoop earrings

★ ALL ABOUT ME ★

★ Favorite school subject: **Spelling**

★ Favorite family recipe: **Momma's sweet potato pudding**

★ Ambition: **To become a teacher**

★ Hobbies: **Jumping rope, gardening, making puppets, and putting on puppet shows**

Lace pantalettes

Bedtime

Winter is chilly in the tiny attic where Addy and Momma live in Philadelphia. Addy is thankful for her flannel nightgown and cozy quilt.

In This Year...

The Civil War has been going on for three years. The North and the South are divided on whether slavery should be legal.

Addy's world

Even in hard times, Addy's family makes time for fun, such as going to the church's summer fair and celebrating birthdays and holidays together.

Tiny berry brooch

A special day
Addy doesn't know her actual birthday, so she chooses one. She picks April 9, the day the war ends. This way, the whole country celebrates with her!

Table set for birthday celebration

Holiday gifts
Addy works at Mrs. Ford's dress shop to earn money for a gift for Momma. She receives a gift, too: a plaid dress to wear on Christmas Day.

SAMANTHA PARKINGTON™

Samantha is growing up under the care of her wealthy grandmother. They live in a time of great change, with new ideas and inventions altering the way people live. Still, Samantha can see that times aren't good for everyone. She tries to help others less fortunate.

Private lessons

Samantha's friend Nellie O'Malley is working as a servant next door and can't go to school. Samantha teaches Nellie to read and write.

ALL ABOUT ME

★ Best friend: **Nellie O'Malley**

★ Favorite ice cream flavor: **Peppermint**

★ Likes: **Painting, paper dolls, ice-skating, and helping others**

★ Dislikes: **Practicing piano and embroidery**

In This Year...

Only men are allowed to vote. Brave women called suffragists fight hard to change that law.

Black Mary Jane shoes

Velvety burgundy purse

Samantha's world

Samantha likes to paint, just as her mother did. Summer trips to Piney Point, Grandmary's summer home in the mountains, give Samantha plenty of inspiration.

Straw hat with ribbon

Pretty picture

On sunny days, Samantha catches butterflies with a net. When it rains, she "captures" them by painting pictures on Grandmary's covered porch.

Palette and paintbrush

Bike and bloomers

As a "proper young lady," Samantha has to wear dresses every day—except when she rides a bicycle! She loves the freedom of riding in her bloomers.

DID YOU KNOW?
Cars were brand new inventions in 1904. Only wealthy families had one.

Checked bloomers

NELLIE O'MALLEY™

Nellie is working as a servant when she meets Samantha Parkington, who lives next door. When Nellie becomes an orphan, Samantha helps Nellie stay strong as she strives to take care of her younger sisters.

White sunhat with blue ribbon

Bedtime

Nellie loves going to her friend Samantha's house for a sleepover. The girls share stories and secrets late into the night.

ALL ABOUT ME

★ Best friend: **Samantha Parkington**

★ Siblings: **Two little sisters, Bridget and Jenny**

★ Dream for the future: **To be a teacher**

★ Skills: **Sewing, singing, and arithmetic**

Purse holds hankie and Irish penny

DID YOU KNOW?

Nellie's nickname is "Miss Nellie O'Malley-All-Mended," because her father taught her how to repair things—even cars!

Nellie's world

Nellie moves in with Samantha when Samantha's aunt and uncle adopt Samantha, Nellie, and her two sisters. Nellie loves her new life but holds onto treasures from her past.

Celtic cross necklace

Hair bow with rhinestones

Finer things

Nellie gets a new wardrobe and fancy accessories when she is adopted. But her prized possession is the cross necklace that belonged to her mother.

In This Year...

In large cities like New York City, illnesses and factory accidents are common, leaving many children orphaned.

Dolled up

Nellie treasures her porcelain doll Lydia—her first doll ever! Samantha gives Nellie the doll to comfort her during hard times.

Shoes with pink ribbon rosettes

REBECCA RUBIN™

My year is 1914

Rebecca will take on any role that brightens people's lives—from helping a friend to gathering around the Sabbath table with her family. She honors her family's Jewish traditions, and she also loves the latest things, like silent movies!

The Sabbath

Every Friday night, Rebecca's family celebrates the Jewish Sabbath with a traditional meal. Rebecca longs for the day when she can light the candles herself, like her older sisters do.

Purse with wrist strap

In This Year...

World War I breaks out in Europe. After that, it is very hard for Jewish families to leave and come to America.

ALL ABOUT ME

★ Family nickname: **Beckie**
★ Favorite book: ***Rebecca of Sunnybrook Farm* by Kate Douglas Wiggin**
★ Favorite subject: **Arithmetic**
★ Hobbies: **Telling jokes, crocheting, singing, and acting**

Rebecca's world

DID YOU KNOW?
Rebecca doesn't go to a movie, or "motion picture show," until she's 10.

Rebecca wants to be an actress, but her parents want her to do something more traditional, such as teaching. But Rebecca never gives up on her dream.

Director's chair

Action!
Rebecca is thrilled to visit a movie studio with her cousin Max, where she gets to see a real director's chair, megaphone, and props.

Title cards

Dressing up
Rebecca loves to dress up, act out plays, and imagine she's a movie star. She can add dramatic music to her scenes by playing records on her phonograph.

Dress-up outfit with golden wings

KIT KITTREDGE™

When Kit's dad loses his business and her family faces hard times during the Great Depression, Kit puts her creativity to work to make things better. She reaches out to help others and discovers that, even in hard times, hope is always worth holding on to.

Cloche hat with ribbon

A nose for news

Kit is tired of hearing about bad news. So she writes her own newspaper at her attic desk, reporting happier news from around her neighborhood.

In This Year...

America is deep in a financial crisis. Many Americans are without jobs, money, and homes.

Cuff bracelet

ALL ABOUT ME

★ Best friend: **Ruthie Smithens**

★ Dream for the future: **To be a newspaper reporter**

★ Favorite baseball player: **Ernie Lombardi of the Cincinnati Reds**

★ Pet: **A Basset Hound named Grace**

Kit's world

DID YOU KNOW?
Kit's real name is Margaret Mildred Kittredge, after her mother and Aunt Millie.

Through challenges and adventures, Kit learns there is more to life than wealth. Even though her family doesn't have much money, Kit knows she has a lot to be grateful for.

Blue cap is a gift from her friend Will

Going to press

Kit types up her news stories on a typewriter. Her news brings a smile to the faces of her readers— her family and their boarders.

Kit's typewriter

Special delivery!

Kit delivers eggs on her scooter to earn extra money. Made from an orange crate and roller skates, the scooter even has room for Kit's dog, Grace.

Kit's brother's old overalls

33

RUTHIE SMITHENS™

My year is 1934

Ruthie may be growing up during the Great Depression, but she loves fairy tales and happy endings. She loves her best friend, Kit Kittredge, too. So when she learns that Kit's family is having trouble paying the mortgage on their house, Ruthie searches for ways to make a real-life happy ending come true.

Pitching in

Ruthie ties on an apron and joins Kit on washday. If one girl does the wash while the other irons, chores will be done in half the time!

Watch from her father

Purse and pretty hankie

In This Year...

President Roosevelt's New Deal is in its second year. This government program was designed to pull America out of the Depression.

ALL ABOUT ME

★ Nickname: **Goofy Ruthie**

★ Dream job: **Princess or movie star**

★ Favorite book: *Grimm's Fairy Tales*

★ Favorite place: **Kit's house, because it's full of interesting boarders!**

Ruthie's world

Velvety ribbon headband

DID YOU KNOW?
Ruthie's father keeps his job at the bank, but she knows most families aren't as lucky as hers.

Ruthie and Kit find ways to celebrate the good times without spending money. They enjoy holiday baking and throw a "penny-pincher birthday party."

Metal table and chairs

Pink glass pitcher and glasses

Home-grown party
Ruthie loves Kit's penny-pincher party! They decorate the table with fresh flowers from the garden. Kit's Aunt Millie gives the girls lessons in planting seeds, too.

Smocked drop-waist dress

From the heart
Homemade gifts and treats are the perfect way for Ruthie to celebrate the holidays with Kit. They can bake for their families—and for other families in need.

MOLLY McINTIRE™

My year is 1944

Navy blue beret

A lively, lovable girl, Molly is growing up during World War II. She misses her father, a doctor who is caring for wounded soldiers overseas. She also struggles with the many changes that the war has brought to America. But through her spirit and resourcefulness, Molly is able to find fun in life on the home front.

School days

Molly's teacher, Miss Campbell, says that going to school is Molly's war duty—that being a good student is as important as being a good soldier. Molly tries her best to pay attention and work hard.

Flared skirt

DID YOU KNOW?

Molly dreads multiplication tests. She gets so nervous, she forgets everything she has learned!

ALL ABOUT ME

★ Family nickname: **Olly Molly**

★ Best friends: **Linda, Susan, and Emily**

★ Best furry friend: **Bennett, a Jack Russell Terrier puppy**

★ Lives in: **Jefferson, Illinois**

Molly's world

Celebrating happy occasions, like birthdays, helps Molly take her mind off the war. Molly also loves activities such as school recitals, tap dance classes, and enjoying the great outdoors at summer camp.

Curvy chrome chairs

Birthday tea party

Molly wants an English tea party for her tenth birthday, which she celebrates with her new English friend, Emily. They serve their chocolate cake on elegant china plates.

In This Year...

Some foods, like butter and cocoa, are hard to get during the war. A chocolate birthday cake is a real treat!

Satin school recital outfit

Making camp

At Camp Gowonagain, Molly and her friends sleep in a canvas tent. Molly borrows her dad's flannel sleeping bag to keep her cozy on cool summer nights.

TENT NO. 6

Shiny shoes with bows

EMILY BENNETT™

Cherry-blossom headband

When her home in London, England, is bombed during World War II, Emily's parents send her to America for safety. She stays with Molly McIntire's family. The girls are from different countries, but they have a lot in common. They both love dogs, and they both worry about loved ones during the war.

ALL ABOUT ME

★ Secret wish: **To have curly hair like an English princess**

★ Secret skill: **Identifying fighter planes**

★ Likes: **Helping Molly with math and Mrs. Gilford in the garden**

Pair of pups

Emily and Molly like pretending they're taking their imaginary dogs for walks outside. On Molly's birthday, each girl gets a real terrier puppy.

T-strap shoes

In This Year...

Thousands of British children are evacuated from London during World War II. Many feel homesick during their time away.

38

Emily's world

DID YOU KNOW?
Emily's toughest day in America is her first day at school. She doesn't like being the center of attention.

Emily tries not to feel homesick, but sometimes it's hard. Her treasures from home comfort her. And Molly cheers her up by teaching her American pastimes, like tap dancing.

World War I identity tags

Home treasures

What reminds Emily of home? The cardigan sweater from Aunt Primrose, a scrapbook of photos, and her grandfather's identity tags from when he was a soldier in World War I.

Snow day

Emily is surprised by how much snow falls in Illinois. She wears a cozy snowsuit to keep warm. Though metal and wood are scarce during the war, she gets to try Molly's old wooden sled.

Tap dance shoes

MARYELLEN LARKIN™

Maryellen is always dreaming up big ideas, even though they sometimes get her into trouble. Her wild imagination helps her stand out from the crowd—and from her five brothers and sisters.

Lacy-knit shrug

★ ALL ABOUT ME ★

- ★ Nickname: **Ellie**
- ★ Siblings: **Joan, Carolyn, Beverly, Tom, and Mikey**
- ★ Favorite TV shows: **Davy Crockett and The Lone Ranger**
- ★ Likes: **Drawing, science experiments, and pretending to be a TV heroine**

Skate on!

When she was seven years old, Maryellen caught a disease called polio. The polio made one of her legs weak, but that doesn't stop Maryellen from running, swimming, and ice-skating.

Striped dress with full skirt

In This Year...

A new vaccine is offered for Polio. Before this, the disease affected thousands of people.

Maryellen's world

DID YOU KNOW?
Maryellen loves pretending she's in a TV show. But when she puts on a show, she gets stage fright!

Whether she's watching TV or playing with friends, Maryellen is always ready for fun. Her playclothes keep her cool in hot, sunny Florida.

TV console with record player

TV dreams

Maryellen likes curling up on the couch to watch her favorite TV shows. She likes inventing her own episodes even more!

At the diner

The Seaside Diner is Maryellen's favorite place to meet her friends. After school, they talk about TV shows they've watched, dance to popular songs on the jukebox, and enjoy tasty burgers and milkshakes.

Denim capris

MELODY ELLISON™

Melody is chosen to sing a solo at her church in Detroit, but she is nervous. When she hears Dr. Martin Luther King Jr. speak at a march for freedom, his words inspire her to lift her own voice in support of equality for all people. It takes courage, but she learns each individual voice really can make a difference.

Cowl collar

Block party

Melody counts down the days until her neighborhood block party. She can't wait to play bingo and eat yummy snacks with her neighbors. She recruits her friends to help her fix up the local park, too.

Bows on side pleats

ALL ABOUT ME

★ Nickname: **Dee-Dee**

★ Best friend: **Her cousin Val**

★ Favorite dessert: **Mommy's triple-chocolate cake**

★ Hobbies: **Singing and gardening**

DID YOU KNOW?
Melody pretends she's a star, singing into her hairbrush like a microphone. But she's actually scared to sing alone in front of a crowd!

Melody's world

Melody loves to spend time with her family. She records music with her brother and attends church with her grandparents every week. They give her a fancy new winter coat for her New Year's Day birthday.

A family trip

Melody packs her red suitcase for a trip to Alabama to visit relatives. While there, she learns more about her family's past when she goes to the farm where her grandparents used to live.

Warm furry hat

Brocade coat

Toiletry case

Big dreams

At night, Melody dreams of equality. She thinks of ways she can use her voice to make a difference.

In This Year...

The long fight for equality leads to the the Civil Rights Act, outlawing racial discrimination.

JULIE ALBRIGHT™

Small side braid

Julie is growing up in San Francisco in the 1970s. It is a time of change in the U.S. and in Julie's own life. Julie finds some changes hard to get used to, like her parents getting divorced. But she discovers that sometimes change is worth fighting for. She campaigns to save endangered animals and to make sure girls have equal opportunities at school.

Save the eagles

By washing cars, Julie and her friend Ivy can raise money to help save endangered eagles. A Volkswagen Beetle is the first car in line!

Bell-bottom jeans

ALL ABOUT ME

★ Favorite colors: **Purple and yellow**

★ Favorite food: **Chocolate fondue**

★ Best friends: **Ivy, T.J., and Nutmeg, her pet rabbit**

★ Best birthday celebration: **A picnic at the beach**

Julie's world

DID YOU KNOW?
Julie's nickname on the basketball court is "Cool Hand Albright" because she passes the ball so swiftly.

Julie's favorite sport is basketball. There is no girls' basketball team at school, so she petitions to be allowed to play on the boys' team.

Speakers built into chair

Chill-out time

After school or basketball practice, Julie relaxes in her stereo egg chair. She can turn on the tunes and put up her feet on her plush orange ottoman.

In This Year...

There is an oil shortage in America. People carpool, walk, or ride bikes to save gas.

Parade bike

Julie is ready to say "Happy Birthday" to America, which is 200 years old in 1976! She rides this red, white, and blue bike in the Bicentennial parade.

Basketball shoes

IVY LING™

In her bustling Chinese American family, Ivy sometimes feels invisible. Her dad works two jobs and her mother is always busy studying. On top of that, Ivy's best friend, Julie, moved to another part of San Francisco! But Ivy learns that by making her own decisions, she can make her own good luck, too.

Chandelier earrings

★ ALL ABOUT ME ★

- ★ Nickname: **Poison Ivy**
- ★ Best friend: **Julie Albright**
- ★ Favorite sport: **Gymnastics**
- ★ Favorite holiday: **Chinese New Year**

Bag made from blue jeans

Forever friends

Ivy sees Julie whenever she comes back to the old neigborhood to stay with her dad. They have sleepovers, shoot hoops, and go shopping—just like old times!

In This Year...

Crafts using recycled materials—such as an old pair of blue jeans—are popular.

Ivy's world

Ivy loves Chinese New Year traditions, from making decorations to watching the dragon parade. The holiday lasts for 15 days and includes visits with family and friends.

DID YOU KNOW?
Ivy's red silk dress is a holiday tradition—her family always buys new clothing for the new year.

Fondue pot

Chocolate fondue

Long forks for dipping

Ivy's family celebrates New Year with traditional Chinese sweets and American sweets, too. Ivy's favorite American treat is chocolate fondue.

Brocade pattern

Parade day

During Chinese New Year, colorful paper lanterns, bright banners, and popping firecrackers decorate the streets of Chinatown. Ivy thinks they look magical.

LINDSEY BERGMAN™

Beaded bobby pin

Lindsey dreams of making the world a better place, but sometimes her best intentions lead her into trouble. But when her brother goes through a tough time, Lindsey steps up and comes through.

Busy bee

Lindsey tries to play matchmaker to her teachers, find her lost dog, and stop the bullying at school. She uses her laptop and notebook to keep track of her plans.

Striped-arm hoodie

In This Year...

Laptop computers are popular, but most Americans don't yet have an Internet connection. Information is transferred on computer disks.

ALL ABOUT ME

★ Extracurricular activity: **Playing trumpet in the school band**

★ Pet: **A dog named Mr. Tiny**

★ Favorite way to get around: **Scooter**

★ Favorite animal: **Dog**

Lindsey's world

Lindsey gets from place to place on her shiny scooter. Her butterfly helmet keeps her safe while she zooms down the sidewalk.

Butterfly helmet

Laptop computer

THURSDAY
10 - 18 - 2001
A 11-30 47

Staying connected

Lindsey takes her laptop computer everywhere. She carries it in a messenger-style bag along with a notebook, pencil, and computer disks.

DID YOU KNOW?
Lindsey's idea to cover ugly trashcans with smiley face stickers backfires when she gets into trouble for damaging property!

Colorful tights

Two-wheeled scooter

KAILEY HOPKINS™

My year is 2003

Sporty Kailey loves living by the sea. When a new development threatens her favorite beach and the creatures living there, Kailey works to save the shoreline. She learns that a person is never too young, or too old, to speak out for what they believe in.

Ruffled embroidered sundress

ALL ABOUT ME

★ Favorite sports: **Boogie boarding and snorkeling**
★ Pet: **Sandy the dog**
★ Favorite place: **The beach**
★ Lives in: **Southern California**

Best friends

Kailey takes her dog, Sandy, wherever she goes. Whether they are out for a walk or surfing the waves together, Sandy and Kailey always have fun.

Woven sandals

In This Year...

California's Long Beach Department of Parks, Recreation and Marine receives a gold-medal award for its public programs.

Kailey's world

DID YOU KNOW?
Kailey and her friend Tess both love the beach, but they disagree about whether putting a shopping mall on part of the beach is a good idea!

Kailey spends all her free time at the beach. Her favorite thing to do is look at the tide pools. Each pool is like its own little world.

Catch a wave

Kailey enjoys riding waves to the shore on her boogie board. It is covered in a silvery starfish design and includes a wrist leash so her board can't be swept away by the waves.

Boogie-board bag

Colorblock wetsuit

Ocean fun

Kailey wears her sparkly bikini when she searches the beach's tide pools for marine creatures. She always makes sure they're safe from harm.

MARISOL LUNA™

Crocheted cap

Marisol loves to dance! So when her parents decide to move to the suburbs of Chicago, she is sad to find that her new neighborhood doesn't have a dance studio. With the help of new friends, Marisol persuades a local dancer to start teaching dance classes.

Jazzed up

Marisol enjoys lots of different types of dance, including jazz and tap. In her shimmery purple costume, Marisol is ready to perform a jazz routine.

Shiny cargo pants

In This Year...

The Joffrey Ballet celebrates its 10th anniversary in Chicago, after moving there from New York City in 1995.

ALL ABOUT ME

★ Pet: **Rascal the cat**

★ Favorite type of dance: **Ballet folklórico (Mexican folk dance)**

★ Motto: **"Never give up your dreams."**

★ School champion at: **Two-Square, a playground game**

Marisol's world

Dancing is close to Marisol's heart, but following her passion can be hard work. No matter what challenges she faces, Marisol always does her best.

Glittery top hat

Purple feather boa

Performance prep

When Marisol has a dance performance, she packs her trunk with all of the supplies she needs to deliver a great show.

AMERICAN GIRL THEATER

Long-sleeved leotard

Fringe skirt

Practice makes perfect

Marisol loves all kinds of dance. She has never taken ballet before and she finds the classes difficult at first. But she keeps practicing and improving.

DID YOU KNOW?
Marisol's neighbor Miss Mendoza, a former professional dancer, inspires and encourages Marisol to keep working at ballet.

Tap shoes

JESS McCONNELL™

My year is **2006**

Loose braids

Jess is excited to leave the United States for the first time and travel to Belize in Central America with her archeologist parents. They spend five months at a dig of ancient Mayan ruins. In Belize, Jess discovers lots of new things about the world—and about herself.

Swing time

Jess enjoys sitting in her swinging chair with Toshi the monkey. Together, they listen to the sounds of the jungle.

Tie-dye print skirt

ALL ABOUT ME

★ Home state: **Michigan**

★ Hobby: **Soccer**

★ Favorite instrument: **Guitar**

★ Foster pet: **Pippi the parrot**

DID YOU KNOW?
Jess has a mix of Japanese, Scottish, and Irish ancestry.

Jess's world

Jess has never traveled far from home before. She is looking forward to an adventure filled with exploring, spotting new animals, and trying things she's never done, such as kayaking.

Belize guidebook

Adventure accessories

Jess can carry everything she needs in her tote bag. It's the best place to keep her passport, a map, a bottle of water, a guidebook, and her butterfly camera while she's exploring.

Long-sleeve swim top

River ready

Jess is always up for a challenge. In Belize, she paddles through river rapids in an inflatable kayak for the first time.

In This Year...

Archeologists discover the earliest example of Mayan writing in a cave. The carefully drawn symbols are likely to be at least 2,200 years old.

Kayaking shoes

NICKI FLEMING™

Nicki loves volunteering for projects at school or on her family's ranch, especially if it means working with animals. Sometimes she takes on more than she can handle, but Nicki always finds a way to make things work.

ALL ABOUT ME

★ Favorite sport: **Skiing**

★ Favorite hobby: **Art**

★ Loves: **Animals**

★ Favorite animals: **Sprocket the puppy and Jackson the horse**

DID YOU KNOW?
Nicki names her twin sisters, Rebecca and Kristine, after her best friends, Becca and Kris.

Cowgirl-style boots

Gala girl

Nicki works hard to make her school's gala event a success. She dresses in her best outfit for the big night, pairing a pretty twill jacket with a floral mesh skirt.

Nicki's world

Nicki spends lots of time outdoors on her Colorado ranch. She especially loves riding her horse, Jackson, in the Rocky Mountains.

Horse tack box

Horse helper
On the ranch, Nicki helps to look after the horses. She grooms them and gives them treats. She stores their supplies in a blue tack box.

Mountain ride
Nicki rides Western-style, using the same type of saddle and bridle that cowboys use.

In This Year...
2007 marks 100 years since conservationists began their campaign to create Rocky Mountain National Park.

NICKI

Chaps protect Nicki's legs when she rides

MIA ST. CLAIR™

Mia loves being on the ice and dreams of one day becoming a professional figure skater. By working hard to improve her skating, Mia knows she can achieve her dream.

On display

Mia's passion for figure skating shows in her bedroom. She decorates her room with skating ribbons and trophies.

In This Year...

Californian figure skater Mirai Nagasu wins gold at the United States Figure Skating Championships held in Minnesota.

Jersey skating skirt

ALL ABOUT ME

★ Favorite activities: **Figure skating and playing hockey with her brothers**

★ Funniest moment: **Skating while dressed as a giant squirrel**

★ Coach's motto: **"Win or lose, always be a good sport."**

Mia's world

DID YOU KNOW?
To help with ice-skating costs, Mia volunteers at the Lucerne Skate Club—the rink where she practices and performs figure skating.

Mia has always played hockey with her brothers, but her passion is for figure skating. Whenever Mia is on the ice, she is practicing to perfect her spins and jumps.

Hair-styling kit

Sparkly mesh sleeves

Perfect ponytail

When it's time for Mia to perform on the ice, she uses tools from her styling kit to create a hairstyle as lovely as her skating outfit.

Hockey practice

Mia puts on her hockey jersey to shoot pucks on the ice with her three hockey-playing brothers.

White figure skates

CHRISSA MAXWELL™

My year is 2009

Chrissa is a creative girl who moves from Iowa to Minnesota with her family. Starting at a new school is hard, and it's even worse when a group of girls called the Mean Bees make Chrissa feel unwelcome. But Chrissa finds the courage to stand strong in the face of bullying.

Snow style

Chrissa's new hometown in Minnesota is a great place for winter sports. Chrissa zips down snowy slopes on her snow tube.

Floral-print wrap dress

DID YOU KNOW?

For her craft projects, Chrissa uses yarn that her nana makes from their pet llamas' wool.

ALL ABOUT ME

★ Favorite sports: **Swimming and diving**

★ Pet: **Starburst, a mini llama**

★ Favorite after-school activities: **Arts and crafts, especially sewing**

Chrissa's world

At first, Chrissa has trouble fitting in at her new school. With encouragement from her best friend back in Iowa, Chrissa joins the school's swim club. It turns out to be a great place to make new friends!

Goggles and swim cap

Knitting needles and yarn

Crafty girl
Chrissa enjoys making handmade gifts for her new friends, Gwen and Sonali. Her craft studio is filled with everything she needs for her sewing and knitting projects.

Sewing machine

In This Year...

In April 2009, the U.S. passes a bill to stop cyberbullying, which includes sending mean messages online.

Dive in
Chrissa is a strong swimmer. She loves competing in swim meets and wearing the swim club's uniform.

SONALI MATTHEWS™

My year is 2009

Silky brown hair

When Sonali's longtime friends, Tara and Jadyn, begin to bully others, Sonali tries to find the courage to stand up and speak out. After Sonali befriends Chrissa and Gwen, the three girls take a stand together against bullying at their school.

ALL ABOUT ME

★ Favorite activities: **Diving and swimming**

★ Favorite pet: **Tofu the dog**

★ New hobby: **Knitting**

★ Nervous habit: **Twisting her hair around her finger**

A picnic

This lake-side party has a purpose—Chrissa, Sonali, and, Gwen discuss ways to stop bullying at school and make it a friendlier place. Their parents join the conversation, too.

Knit tunic

Denim capris

In This Year...

American Girl declares May 1, 2009, to be Stop the Bullying Day. Thousands of children sign pledges to stand up to bullying.

GWEN THOMPSON™

Gwen's family has fallen on hard times and Gwen is being bullied at school. When Chrissa befriends shy Gwen, she comes out of her shell. With Chrissa by her side, Gwen finds her confidence—and her voice.

Stronger together

These three girls learn that when it comes to standing up to bullies, friends are stronger when they stand together.

Eyelet lace dress

★ ALL ABOUT ME ★

★ Favorite animal: **Chrissa's pet llama, Starburst**

★ New hobby: **Swimming**

★ New job: **Assistant manager for the swim team**

Braided sandals

LANIE HOLLAND™

Dragonfly headband

Lanie loves science, wildlife, and the outdoors. She longs to explore the world outside, but the rest of her family prefers to stay indoors. After her Aunt Hannah encourages Lanie to start gardening and bird-watching, Lanie realizes that outdoor adventure can be found close to home.

Striped rugby dress

Sunny slumber

When the sun is shining Lanie loves to hang out in her hammock. From here she can quietly spot birds and animals to sketch in her nature journal.

ALL ABOUT ME

★ Favorite subject: **Science**
★ Pet: **Lulu the lop-eared bunny**
★ Favorite hobbies: **Gardening and sketching**
★ Dream: **To travel around the world helping protect nature and wildlife**
★ Best friend: **Dakota**

DID YOU KNOW?

Lanie's best friend Dakota is also a nature lover. She visits the jungles of Indonesia, helping her father rescue orangutans.

Lanie's world

Lanie loves camping! Whether pitching a tent in her own backyard or staying overnight in her aunt's camper, Lanie is always well prepared.

Sleeping bag

Knit scarf

Gear to go
With a sleeping bag, camp cup, teapot, and more, Lanie has all the supplies she needs to camp out in comfort.

In This Year...
Scientists discover a new species of bird called a Limestone Leaf Warbler in Vietnam and Laos.

Bird watching guide

Happy camper
Lanie's aunt's camper is the perfect vehicle for an outdoor adventure. It provides a cute and cozy place to eat, sleep, and shower after a day of exploring.

KANANI AKINA™

Hibiscus flower clip

Living on the Hawaiian island of Kaua'i, Kanani is filled with the aloha spirit. She loves to make visitors feel welcome. Kanani works at her family's business, Akina's Shave Ice and Sweet Treats. She also helps protect the Hawaiian monk seal.

Painted Hawaiian necklace

ALL ABOUT ME

★ Best friend: **Celina**

★ Proudest moment: **Rescuing a baby monk seal**

★ Enjoys: **Greeting customers at the shave ice shop**

★ Pets: **Jinx the rooster, Barksee the dog, and Mochi the goat**

Cool treats

On sunny days, Kanani helps tourists and beachgoers beat the heat with tasty scoops of shave ice from her family's stand.

Muumuu, a traditional Hawaiian dress

In This Year...

The National Marine Fisheries Service propose a new plan to help protect Hawaiian monk seals.

Kanani's world

DID YOU KNOW?
Kanani works hard to tell people about endangered Hawaiian monk seals. She raises money for them, too.

Kanani loves to share the wonders of her island with visitors. When her cousin Rachel comes from the mainland to stay with the Akinas, Kanani takes her to a feast called a luau, where she performs in a hula show.

"Aloha" greeting card

Aloha!

mochi

pineapple

Sweet send-off

Kanani fills a pretty woven gift box with lots of delicious sweet treats from her parents' store. She gives the gift to Rachel as a reminder of the island.

Flowery lei

Hula show outfit

Catch a wave

One of Kanani's favorite sports is paddleboarding. Standing on top of her board, she can explore the ocean and sea coves, looking for monk seals.

67

MCKENNA BROOKS™

Star necklace from Grandma

McKenna excels in gymnastics. As she enters fourth grade, however, balancing sports with schoolwork is a challenge. When her grades start to slip, she has to find a way to keep up. A tutor helps her realize that she can use her strengths as a gymnast to succeed in the classroom, too.

Walk in the rain

McKenna's dog, Cooper, is always ready for a walk—even in the rain! There are lots of drizzly days in Seattle, but that doesn't stop McKenna from heading outside with her pup.

Gymnastics bag

In This Year...

The 2012 Olympic Games are held in London, United Kingdom. American Gabby Douglas wins gold for best all-around gymnast.

ALL ABOUT ME

★ Best friends: **Sierra and Josie**

★ Cutest pets: **Cooper the dog and Polka Dot the hamster**

★ Gymnastics idol: **Coach Isabelle Manning**

★ Newest hobby: **Helping at the horseback riding center**

McKenna's world

McKenna works hard to try to make the Shooting Stars competitive gymnastics team, but she has even bigger dreams. She hopes to win Olympic gold someday!

Performance leotard

Poetry journal

In the bag
McKenna keeps everything she needs in her sports bag, including a journal where she writes poetry. The journal is a gift from her tutor.

Rhythmic gymnastics wand

Balancing act
The balance beam is one of McKenna's favorite events, until a scary fall shakes her confidence. She has to find the courage to get back up again.

DID YOU KNOW?
McKenna has five-year-old twin sisters, Maisey and Mara. They want to be gymnasts, too!

SAIGE COPELAND™

Whether drawing, painting, or sketching, creative Saige expresses herself through her art. With her school art classes under threat, Saige learns how to put her creative talents to use. With help from her grandmother and friends, Saige speaks out to save the art classes.

Up, up, and away

Saige and her dad love soaring high above the mountains in a hot-air balloon. From the sky, they can see all of the beauty New Mexico has to offer.

DID YOU KNOW?
Saige's home of Albuquerque, New Mexico, is known as the hot-air balloon capital of the world.

Colorful canvas purse

ALL ABOUT ME

★ Favorite class: **Art**
★ Favorite pastime: **Horseback riding**
★ Worst fear: **Speaking in public**
★ Pet: **A dog named Sam**
★ Talent: **Painting horse portraits**

Saige's world

Whether trail riding with her grandmother or painting the beautiful landscapes of New Mexico, Saige loves the great outdoors.

Paintbrush holder

Work of art

To create the perfect picture, Saige first draws in her sketch pad. Once she has a rough drawing, she sets up her easel and brushes to paint her work of art.

Belt with cowgirl-style buckle

Ranch rider

Saige's grandmother, Mimi, has many horses on her ranch. Named after the famous artist, Picasso is Saige's favorite horse.

ISABELLE PALMER™

Nine-year-old Isabelle is a dancer attending her first year at the Anna Hart School of the Arts in Washington, DC. While she loves to perform, Isabelle's nerves sometimes get the better of her, making her worry if ballet is really for her. Learning to believe in herself, Isabelle discovers her own way to shine.

Flutter sleeve

Practice makes perfect

Isabelle likes to add a bit of shine to her performance, even in dance class. Her wrap skirt with pink and purple sequins makes Isabelle really sparkle!

ALL ABOUT ME

★ Nicknames: **Iz and Izzie**

★ Loves: **Ballet**

★ Hobbies: **Sewing and designing dance costumes**

★ Best friends: **Luisa and Gabriel**

Sparkly shoes

DID YOU KNOW?

To help perfect her turns, Isabelle likes to pretend she's skipping and spinning across water.

Isabelle's world

Isabelle is creative in more ways than one. When she's not rehearsing and performing, Isabelle makes her own costumes. Wearing her own designs gives Isabelle a confidence boost on stage.

Ballet barre

Pink sequins

Ready to dance
When it's time to practice her pliés, Isabelle uses her ballet barre, yoga mat, and accessories to stretch and warm up.

DID YOU KNOW?
A family outing to see the waterlilies at an aquatic garden inspires Isabelle's ballet dress design.

Sparkle and shine
Isabelle and her mom make costumes for the school's Autumn Festival. Isabelle makes this bright pink performance outfit covered with eye-catching sparkles for a shimmering performance.

Floaty tulle

GRACE THOMAS™

A French beret

Grace loves to bake! She can't wait to go to Paris to visit her aunt and uncle's bakery, called a *pâtisserie*. Being away from her friends all summer is hard, but Grace brings back lots of ideas for setting up a bakery with them when she returns.

ALL ABOUT ME

★ Best friends: **Maddy and Ella**

★ Favorite accessory: **A new charm bracelet**

★ Sweetest pet: **Bonbon, the French bulldog**

★ Favorite hobby: **Baking, but it's more than a hobby—it's a business!**

Cart for tarts

A pastry cart means Grace can take her baked goods on the road, along with her favorite baking assistant: Bonbon.

Stylish ankle boots

In This Year...

TV cooking shows for kids, such as MasterChef Junior, are very popular.

74

Grace's world

Grace enjoys biking around Paris with her mom, especially when they stop for lunch at an outdoor café. The sights, smells, and sounds all around her inspire big ideas!

Bow-shaped earrings

Menu board

French treats

Today's special
Grace can't always pronounce the French treats on the menu, but she's willing to try them all!

DID YOU KNOW?
Grace names her own business "La Petite Pâtisserie," inspired by the *pâtisseries* she visits in Paris.

Apron-style dress

Baking buddies
Working with friends is fun, but it isn't always easy. Back home, Grace and her friends learn to combine their talents in creative ways.

LEA CLARK™

Hazel eyes

Traveling to Brazil to visit her brother is a dream come true for Lea. She's a little nervous, but armed with her travel journal and her grandma's compass necklace, she's determined to push past her fears and dive into adventure. She can't wait to see the beautiful beaches and photograph animals in the rainforest!

ALL ABOUT ME

★ Role model: **Grandma Ama**
★ Best friends: **Abby and Camila**
★ Favorite pet: **Ginger the turtle**
★ Favorite hobby: **Photography—especially after winning third place in a magazine contest!**

Canvas messenger bag

DID YOU KNOW?

Lea is one-eighth Brazilian. Her great-grandpa moved to the U.S. from Brazil when he was a boy.

Braided belt

Party dress

Lea sees many Brazilian women wearing traditional white dresses. She celebrates her trip with a white dress of her own, which will always remind Lea of her time in Brazil.

Lea's world

Lea and her brother love exploring in Brazil. At the beach they snorkel, kayak, and even watch baby sea turtles hatch. In the rainforest, they are amazed by all the wildlife they can see up close.

Under the waves

Lea's ocean kayak has a clear bottom so that she can see the fish and coral reef in the water below.

> Collapsible sail

> Snorkeling fins

Rainforest lullaby

Lea stays overnight in a pretty rainforest house. After a day of hiking, she relaxes in the loft bed as the sounds of the forest lull her to sleep.

In This Year...

Many people visit Brazil for the 2016 Summer Olympic Games. Ecotourism trips into the rainforest are also very popular.

GABRIELA McBRIDE™

Creative Gabriela loves performing and the arts—especially poetry. But having a stutter means expressing herself isn't always easy. Gabriela works hard to follow her passion, and learns that by speaking out she can help others, too.

Rising star

Rehearsing for her many performances takes a lot of hard work. Gabriela's stretchy practice outfit keeps her comfortable dancing for hours at a time.

Comfortable leggings

High-top sneakers

DID YOU KNOW?

Poetry is so close to Gabriela's heart that she names her cat Maya, after poet Maya Angelou.

ALL ABOUT ME

★ Nickname: **Gabby**

★ Favorite activities: **Dancing and writing poetry**

★ Proudest moment: **Performing a poem without missing a beat**

Gabriela's world

DID YOU KNOW?
Gabriela has been on stage many times, but she still gets nervous. Before each show she rubs the curtain for luck.

All of Gabriela's hard work pays off when it's time to perform. She loves putting on her costume and getting on stage.

Shoulder bag

Rehearsal essentials

Gabriela has the perfect bag for rehearsals—it's shaped like a boom box. In it she always packs water, snacks, hair accessories, and adhesive bandages.

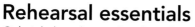

Sequined top

On tape

Gabriela records rhythms for her poetry performances on an electronic drum kit. A sturdy case keeps her equipment safe.

Silver jazz shoes

TENNEY GRANT™

Tenney plays the guitar and writes her own songs. She loves to play for others and share the music that's in her heart. Tenney dreams of making it big one day, but she is determined to stay true to herself and her music in the process.

Denim vest

DID YOU KNOW?
Tenney works at her mom's food truck. Her favorite snack is her mom's famous Nashville hot chicken.

Backstage
Before Tenney performs, she gets ready in a backstage dressing room. She feels just like the big stars she sees on stage in her hometown of Nashville, Tennessee.

Flower-decorated guitar

ALL ABOUT ME

★ Favorite activities: **Writing songs and playing music**

★ Prized possession: **Her trusty guitar**

★ Favorite songwriting spot: **In her family's backyard**

★ Pet: **Waylon, her golden retriever**

Tenney's world

It takes a lot of grit and hard work to make it as a performer. Fortunately, there's time for fun, too. When she gets together with her best friend Jaya, Tenney knows they will have a good time whatever they do.

Wide brim hat

Southern snacks

For an afternoon in the park with her friends, Tenney packs a Southern-style picnic. Her floral picnic blanket is perfect for spreading out on the grass.

Picnic blanket with carry handle

DID YOU KNOW?
"Tenney" is short for Tennyson, after the famous British poet Alfred, Lord Tennyson.

Eyelet lace shorts

The band

When Tenney performs, her band partner Logan plays drums. Tenney feels less nervous with Logan on stage— she knows that she can count him to keep a steady rhythm.

Z YANG™

13-year-old Z loves telling stories through her videos and sharing them with family and friends. But sometimes their feedback can make her feel a little disheartened. Z learns that to be a true filmmaker, she needs to trust her instincts and share her unique take on life.

Camera T-shirt

ALL ABOUT ME

★ Pet: **Popcorn the Dalmatian**

★ Favorite activities: **Filming and editing videos, watching movies, and eating buttery popcorn**

★ First video: **A stop-motion animation film featuring Kit Kittredge**

On the go

Z is always on the lookout for a new story to turn into a video. On her three-wheeled scooter, she can get to where she needs to be quickly.

DID YOU KNOW?

Z earns a chance to make a documentary for a film festival. This could be her big break!

Sparkly shoes

Z's world

Not only does Z have a nose for a story, she is a technology whiz, too. She can operate several different kinds of camera and uses editing equipment with ease.

Scarf worn as a headband

Camera club

Z uses a mounted camera, a digital camcorder, and her smartphone to record the things she sees. She can transfer all of the images onto her computer for editing.

Tripod holds pretend smartphone

Comfortable checked shirt

DID YOU KNOW?
Some of Z's first videos were inspired by real girls using their American Girl dolls to create stop-motion videos.

Editing suite

Back in her bedroom, Z uses editing equipment and creative thinking to turn her video footage into finished films.

Chapter 2
Pet pals

Whether doting on dogs, caring for cats, or sharing their hearts with horses, girls know the importance of looking after all kinds of animals—and having fun with them, too.

STEPS HIGH

DID YOU KNOW?
Steps High gets her name because she "steps high," or prances, when she gets excited.

Kaya's beloved horse, Steps High, is a beautiful Appaloosa mare. Steps High chooses Kaya. When the horse sees Kaya for the first time, she nudges her head against Kaya's leg. Kaya knows from that day on that Steps High will be hers.

Saddle pad

Together again

When Kaya and Steps High are reunited after her mare is captured, Kaya finds that Steps High has a foal. She names him Sparks Flying. Now Kaya has two horses to love!

Fringed blanket

Spotted Appaloosa coat

ALL ABOUT ME

★ Personality: **Graceful and strong**

★ Favorite activity: **Running as fast as the wind**

★ Proudest moment: **Saving Kaya's sister Speaking Rain from the river**

PENNY

Penny is a Thoroughbred mare who is mistreated by her owner, Jiggy Nye. When Felicity Merriman first meets Penny, she decides right away to help Penny escape from her cruel owner. Thanks to Felicity, the mare gains her independence at a time when America is fighting for its own.

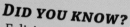

DID YOU KNOW?
Felicity gives Penny her name. It is short for inde-PEN-dence, and celebrates Penny's spirit.

ALL ABOUT ME

★ Personality: **Spirited**

★ Favorite treat: **Sugar**

★ Bravest moment: **Leaping a fence to freedom**

Royal blue saddle blanket

To the ball
By proudly pulling the carriage, Penny gets to go to the Christmas Eve ball with Felicity and her friend Elizabeth. Felicity's greatest holiday gift is having Penny by her side.

Adjustable stirrups

INKPOT

Caroline Abbott has loved her pet cat, Inkpot, since Papa brought him home as a tiny stray kitten. His rumbling purr comforts her when she's scared or lonely. Inkpot sticks close to Caroline when she sits by the hearth or sleeps in her bed—until the urge to chase mice strikes!

White patch on chest

Bedtime buddies

Inkpot likes to curl up in Caroline's canopy bed. When he wants to go outside, he wakes her with a gentle touch of his paw on her cheek.

DID YOU KNOW?

According to Caroline's father, sailors believe black cats are good luck!

SOMBRITA

When Florecita the goat dies and leaves a tiny orphan behind, Josefina Montoya is determined to raise her. She names the little goat Sombrita, and gives her a silver bell so she can hear her wherever she goes. Together, they explore the hills near their home on a New Mexican rancho.

Black stripe down back

ALL ABOUT ME

★ Personality: **Frisky and playful**

★ Favorite place to be petted: **Behind the ears**

★ Favorite chores: **Fetching water and herbs with Josefina**

Silver bell

Little helper

After Josefina finds baby Sombrita and nurses her back to health, Josefina realizes she wants be a healer like her aunt. Sombrita stays by Josefina's side when she collects healing herbs from the garden.

COCHON

Cécile Rey's colorful parrot, Cochon, has brilliant red and green feathers and a loud squawk. Cécile has to be careful what she says around him—he often repeats people's words! He even knows how to say, "Pecans, girl! Pecans!" to demand his favorite treat.

DID YOU KNOW?
Cochon means "pig" in French—which suits this hungry parrot!

In the parlor
Cochon keeps Cécile company while she reads or writes letters. When he gets too noisy, she puts a blanket over his cage to quiet him.

Metal birdcage

ALL ABOUT ME

★ Personality: **Loud, bold, and noisy**

★ Favorite snack: **Pecans**

★ Favorite place: **Cécile's shoulder**

★ Favorite activity: **Mimicking someone's words**

ARGOS

Ever since Marie-Grace Gardner was very young, her dog Argos has been her constant companion. He has huggable shaggy fur and a curly tail. His size scares some people when they first meet him, including Marie-Grace's friend, Cécile. But Cécile soon learns that this enormous dog is a little sweetheart.

ALL ABOUT ME

★ Personality: **Friendly, loyal, and protective**

★ Breed: **Bouvier des Flandres**

★ Favorite place: **By Marie-Grace's side**

Buddy guard

Whether Marie-Grace is walking to her singing lessons or heading off to the market, she's never alone. Argos walks close by to protect her, especially on busy streets.

DID YOU KNOW?

Uncle Luc rescued Argos when he was a puppy and gave him to Marie-Grace.

Shaggy gray fur

MISSY

Kirsten Larson's cat, Missy, is one of her favorite animals on the farm. When Missy has kittens, one is so tiny that its heartbeat feels like the flutter of butterfly wings. Kirsten falls in love with the little kitten. It has a gray coat and bright green eyes, just like its mother.

ALL ABOUT ME

★ Personality: **Sweet, strong, and protective**

★ Best feature: **Super-soft gray fur**

★ Favorite activity: **Keeping the barn mouse-free**

★ Favorite hangout: **A pile of straw in the warm barn**

Pink-tipped ears

Soft furry paws

Cozy quilt

Kirsten helps Missy care for her tiniest kitten. She keeps it warm in her lap while she works on her quilt. The finished quilt keeps them all cozy at bedtime, too.

DID YOU KNOW?

Only one of Missy's kittens is all gray like her. The others are black and white or gray and white.

SUNNY

Sunny, a canary, belongs to Addy Walker's new neighbor and friend, M'dear. When Sunny cocks his head and puffs out his chest, he sings a special song full of hope and happiness. Sunny's song reminds Addy to let her own spirit sing, too, even when times are hard.

DID YOU KNOW?
For Addy's birthday, M'dear gives her two of Sunny's feathers to pin in her hair.

ALL ABOUT ME

★ Personality: **Bright and cheerful**
★ Favorite activity: **Singing**
★ Favorite place: **On the perch, overlooking a room**

A special bird

Addy first meets M'Dear when she goes to take a closer look at Sunny. The wise older woman soon becomes her friend. Addy loves to visit M'Dear and hear Sunny's joyful song.

Wooden perch

JIP

Jip is a playful cocker spaniel who brings plenty of excitement to Samantha Parkington's life. Even though he sometimes leaves muddy paw prints on her pinafore, Jip's sweetness makes up for it every time.

Long, droopy ears

Pup at the party

Jip meets Samantha when Uncle Gard and Aunt Cornelia bring him to her birthday party. Even though Jip runs off with Samantha's new teddy bear, Samantha can't help but love him anyway.

ALL ABOUT ME

★ Personality: **Frisky, playful, and mischievous**

★ Eye color: **Brown**

★ Favorite activities: **Swimming and playing with Samantha**

★ Favorite hangout: **Grammercy Park**

Soft, silky fur

REBECCA'S KITTENS

When a neighbor's cat goes missing, Rebecca Rubin finds the sneaky feline in the basement of her apartment building—along with two baby kittens! Rebecca cares for them while their owner, Mr. Rossi, recovers from a winter cold.

Not so sleepy

The kittens have a sleepover at Rebecca's. They play with the tassels on her pillow before curling up to sleep.

Green eyes

Amber eyes

DID YOU KNOW?
The kittens' mother's name is Pasta because she prefers to eat spaghetti over mice.

GRACE

ALL ABOUT ME

★ Personality: **Lazy but lovable**

★ Favorite activity: **Chasing chickens—or just sleeping outside their coop**

★ Best friend: **Kit**

During the Great Depression when many people are out of work, Grace the basset hound is abandoned by an owner who can't afford to feed her. Luckily, Kit Kittredge finds the hungry hound and brings her home.

DID YOU KNOW?
This basset hound is so clumsy that Kit's aunt Millie jokes that there is only one name for her: Grace!

Droopy ears and eyes

Special delivery
When Kit delivers eggs in her neighborhood, Grace goes along for the ride. There's a special place for Grace to sit in Kit's homemade scooter.

Adorable freckles

BENNETT & YANK

These Jack Russell terriers belong to Molly McIntire and her friend Emily Bennett, who comes to stay with the McIntires to escape bombing in London during World War II.

A puppy party
Bennett and Yank are the biggest and best surprises on Molly's tenth birthday. They join Molly and Emily for an English teatime birthday party.

Emily's puppy Yank

Molly's puppy Bennett

ALL ABOUT US

★ Personalities: **Smart, athletic, and mischievous**

★ Favorite activities: **Performing tricks and playing fetch and tug-of-war**

★ Favorite things to chew: **Paper dolls, pillows, and schoolbooks**

SCOOTER

A lovable old dachshund, Scooter is Maryellen Larkin's constant companion. With his short legs and roly-poly body, he waddles more than he walks! He co-stars in her made-up television shows, but he makes an even better audience. He settles right into the nearest comfortable spot, and then he's all ears.

ALL ABOUT ME

★ Personality: **Sleepy, sweet, and sometimes stubborn**
★ Favorite activity: **Napping**
★ Favorite hangout: **The closest shady place**

Soft tan fur

Bedtime buddies

At nighttime, Scooter climbs into bed with Maryellen. He might snore a little, but he knows she won't mind.

Pretty patterned collar

DID YOU KNOW?

Dachshunds have a loud voice—and they enjoy using it. Scooter barks along with children, train whistles, and even the doorbell.

Bo

Like his owner, Melody Ellison, this terrier has an ear for music. When he howls along to songs, Bo has perfect pitch. He's perfectly behaved when he goes on visits with Melody. He wags his tail politely but doesn't bark—unless someone plays music. Then he has to join in!

Soft, fluffy ears

DID YOU KNOW?
Bo was named "Bojangles" after the tap dancer Bill "Bojangles" Robinson. Bo doesn't dance, but he sure can sing!

Collar and leash

Bark for the park

When Bo and Melody walk past a neglected park, he inspires Melody to fix it up. He barks as if to say, "Do something!" and Melody listens.

NUTMEG

Nutmeg is Julie Albright's lop-eared bunny. Julie's mom's new apartment doesn't allow pets, so Nutmeg lives at Julie's dad's house. Julie gives Nutmeg extra love and attention when she stays with her dad.

DID YOU KNOW?
Rabbits can learn to respond to their names as well as to simple commands such as "Come!"

Floppy ears

Bunny in a basket
Nutmeg snuggles with Julie before bed each night, but she has her own basket for sleeping in. With its high sides, Nutmeg feels safe and snug.

Rattan basket with soft, round pillow

ALL ABOUT ME

★ Personality: **Calm and snuggly**
★ Favorite activity: **Cuddling in Julie's lap**
★ Favorite foods: **Crisp carrots and apple peels**
★ Favorite hangout: **The laundry basket or the hutch in the backyard**

SANDY

Sandy is a golden retriever who lives in California with her owner, Kailey Hopkins. A true beach dog, Sandy enjoys the sand and surf almost as much as Kailey does. If Kailey splashes into the ocean, Sandy is sure to dive in, too.

ALL ABOUT ME

★ Personality: **Playful, curious, and athletic**

★ Favorite activity: **Chasing waves and digging holes in the sand**

★ Favorite hangout: **In the surf or snoozing on a beach towel**

DID YOU KNOW?
Golden retrievers have coats that repel water. No wonder Sandy can play in the ocean for hours and never get cold.

Lavender bandanna

Beach buddy
While Kailey snorkels or boogie boards, Sandy takes a swim—or a roll in the sand.

Strong legs for swimming

RASCAL

DID YOU KNOW?
Himalayan cats need daily brushing. Rascal doesn't like being brushed, so Marisol has to work hard to get the job done.

A fluffy Himalayan cat, Rascal showed up on Marisol Luna's doorstep one rainy night. Ever since then, he's been her best friend—making her laugh with his antics and making her worry when he wanders away and doesn't come straight back home. He prances instead of walks and is full of personality.

ALL ABOUT ME

★ Personality: **Lazy by day, active by night**
★ Favorite activities: **Climbing, chasing birds, and watching Marisol dance**
★ Favorite hangouts: **Curled up inside Marisol's dance bag**

Bright blue eyes

Out for a stroll

Rascal loves being outside. When Marisol heads to dance lessons, he tags along for a while—until he spots a bird to watch.

102

SPROCKET

A service dog in training, Sprocket tries to listen to his trainer, Nicki Fleming. But he's still young and still learning, so he sometimes makes mistakes. No one knows his breed. Australian shepherd? Border collie? Bernese mountain dog? Maybe all of the above! But one thing is certain: Nicki adores him.

DID YOU KNOW?

Sprocket, like many service dogs, comes from a shelter. He has an important job to do, but he gets a forever home, too.

Plenty of pockets

When he's out and about, Sprocket wears his service-dog vest. It has lots of pockets so he can carry things for his owner. Nicki keeps his treats in there, too.

ALL ABOUT ME

★ Personality: **Smart, curious, and sweet**

★ Favorite activity: **Going on long walks**

★ Favorite hangout: **On Nicki's bed, as a special treat**

Collar with an "S" tag

JACKSON

A handsome buckskin horse, Jackson lives on a Colorado ranch with his owner, Nicki Fleming. Her family keeps lots of horses. But since Jackson belongs to Nicki, he gets special treatment. In return, he's a steady friend who helps her cope with her changing family and friendships.

ALL ABOUT ME

★ Personality: **Sweet, steady, and strong**

★ Favorite activities: **Going for a gallop and being groomed**

★ Favorite snacks: **Apples, carrots, and oats**

★ Favorite place: **A mountain meadow in the spring**

Western-style saddle

Removable bridle

DID YOU KNOW?
"Buckskin" is a color of horse, not a breed. Nicki thinks Jackson's golden coat is gorgeous, especially in sunlight.

Out for a walk
Jackson loves walking through the woods and fields just as much as Nicki does. Up in the saddle, Nicki feels as though she can see for miles.

STARBURST

Named for the way she "bursts" into Chrissa Maxwell's life one summer morning, Starburst is a mini llama. She's a special gift from Chrissa's grandmother, who has two llamas—Cosmos and Checkers. Starburst is just a little baby, but she's big on personality!

DID YOU KNOW?

Crias, or baby llamas, can walk within a few hours of being born. Chrissa is lucky enough to see Starburst take her first steps.

Woven halter and lead

ALL ABOUT ME

★ Personality: **Curious, mischievous, sweet, and energetic**
★ Favorite activity: **Exploring the world outside**
★ Favorite place: **Nestled beside her momma, Cosmos**

Guest of honor

When Chrissa and her parents throw a party at their house, who bursts onto the scene, ready to play? It's Starburst, of course!

Fleece blanket with pockets

LULU

A pet rabbit who loves to be outdoors, Lulu enjoys sunning on the deck or taking walks around the neighborhood with her owner, Lanie Holland. When Lanie clips a leash on to Lulu's walking vest, Lulu jumps for joy. Lulu leads the way outside, stopping to sniff the plants—or sometimes to chase the neighbor's cat!

ALL ABOUT ME

★ Personality: **Curious and friendly**

★ Favorite treats: **Fresh grass, vegetables, and alfalfa pellets**

★ Favorite hideout: **The crook of Lanie's elbow**

DID YOU KNOW?
Some rabbit owners take classes on leash-training their rabbits. Lanie teaches Lulu herself, first getting her used to the leash indoors.

Fun outdoors
Lanie takes Lulu for walks around the bedroom before heading outside. When Lulu does a happy leap in the backyard, Lanie knows Lulu loves to be outdoors as much as she does.

Orange leash

LANIE'S WILD ANIMALS

When Lanie goes hiking or camping, she keeps an eye out for wild animals. Will she spot a red fox, a gray squirrel with a bushy tail, a ring-tailed raccoon, or a snowy owl? Thanks to the wildflower garden she plants, she sees plenty of Monarch butterflies—right in her own backyard.

DID YOU KNOW?
Monarch butterflies lay their eggs on milkweed. Lanie plants it to invite monarchs into her garden.

Looking up

Lying in her hammock, Lanie looks out for wildlife. To remember what she sees, she records everything in her nature journal.

Raccoon

Snowy owl

Red fox

Gray squirrel

BARKSEE

This friendly tan-and-white mutt lives with his owner, Kanani Akina, on the Hawaiian island of Kaua'i. Although his name has the word "bark" in it, he only barks to alert Kanani to unusual sounds and sights—like the baby monk seal stranded on the beach who needs their help.

DID YOU KNOW?

Kanani's family rescued Barksee from an animal shelter. He was scrawny and scared, but they helped him become healthy and happy again.

ALL ABOUT ME

★ Personality: **Sweet and friendly**

★ Favorite activities: **Going for walks and barking at birds**

★ Least favorite activity: **Taking a bath**

★ Best friends: **Jinx, the rooster, and Mochi, the goat**

Warm brown eyes

A private paradise

Barksee loves running along the beach with Kanani during their afternoon walks. Sometimes they have the whole beach to themselves.

COOPER

A young goldendoodle, Cooper has the caramel-colored hair of a golden retriever and the curls of a poodle. He has as much energy as his owner, McKenna Brooks. So when she injures herself doing gymnastics, he knows how hard it is for her to rest. He stays by her side until she heals.

DID YOU KNOW?
All puppies need something to chew. When McKenna runs out of puppy chews, Cooper chews her gymnastics grips instead.

Under the bed
Some dogs love hanging out on beds. Cooper's favorite place is underneath McKenna's loft bed, where he keeps her company while she reads or does homework.

ALL ABOUT ME

★ Personality: **Loveable and loyal**

★ Smallest friend: **McKenna's hamster, Polka Dot**

★ Favorite activity: **Going for walks and chasing squirrels**

Curly caramel-colored fur

PICASSO

Picasso the horse belongs to Saige Copeland's grandma, Mimi, but he has a special bond with Saige. She has ridden him since she was small and he is always gentle with her. So when Mimi asks Saige to ride Picasso and lead an upcoming parade, she says, "yes!"

Bridle with silver decoration

Colorful saddle blanket

DID YOU KNOW?
Picasso is a Spanish Barb horse, a rare breed brought to America by Spanish soldiers and explorers in the 1500s.

A shared view
Saige thinks New Mexico looks even more beautiful when she explores it on horseback with Picasso. Sometimes Mimi saddles up another horse and rides with them.

SAM

Saige's dog, Sam, is a shaggy Border Collie mix. He helps Saige make friends with her new neighbor, Gabi. Sam gets along with everyone—except his brother, Rembrandt, who lives with Saige's grandma, Mimi.

Shaggy fur

Leash

Outdoor adventures

Going for walks is one of Sam's favorite things to do. Saige takes him out every morning and evening and sometimes on special trips for picnics.

ALL ABOUT ME

★ Personality: **Friendly and full of energy**

★ Secret talent: **Jumping fences**

★ Favorite meal: **Breakfast, because Saige shares her toast**

★ Favorite painting: **The one Saige painted of him**

TUTU

Isabelle Palmer's kitten got her name because she's as fluffy as a tutu. This diva can leap through the air as high as any ballerina—especially if there's a ribbon dangling overhead. She's also very good at keeping Isabelle and her sister, Jade, on their toes with her antics.

ALL ABOUT ME

★ Personality: **Sometimes sweet and cuddly, sometimes loud and demanding**

★ Most important job: **Waking up Isabelle in the morning**

★ Favorite hideout: **Isabelle's bag**

Sew tempting

Tutu dreams of having Isabelle's sewing room to herself. From long ribbons to measuring tape, there are so many things for a kitten to play with.

Sparkly personalized collar

DID YOU KNOW?

Tutu was a gift for Isabelle's mother, but she prefers to sleep with Isabelle and her sister, Jade.

BONBON

This French bulldog is living on the streets of Paris, France, when Grace Thomas finds her. Grace calls the pup "Bonbon" because, like the French treat, she's a little rough on the outside, but as sweet as chocolate on the inside. When Bonbon wags her tail, Grace knows the name will stick!

DID YOU KNOW?
Grace's cousin, Sylvie, calls Bonbon *petite chienne* [puh-teet shee-an], which means "little dog" in French.

ALL ABOUT ME

★ Personality: **Street-smart, playful, and super sweet**

★ Favorite activities: **Chasing cats**

★ Favorite hangout: **Outside the *pâtisserie* door**

"Pirate's patch" of black fur

Red collar and leash

Puppy training
Bonbon has to learn how to walk on a leash. When she strains at it, Grace makes her walk nicely, by Grace's side. Then Bonbon gets a treat.

COCONUT

Coconut the pup is a West Highland Terrier, often called a "Westie." This frisky pup loves joining in activities and is the best furry friend a girl could ask for. Coconut can sniff out style and loves to play dress-up in cute clothes and costumes. With so much energy used on all her adventures, naps are her favorite downtime.

DID YOU KNOW?
Coconut is a pup with many interests—snowboarding, agility tracks, gardening, and lots more! She loves to try new things in the name of fun.

Reversible bed

Colorful dog tag

Cuddly blanket

Coconut

Purple water bowl

Bouncy chew toy

water

Merry days

Coconut loves to celebrate the holidays with her best friend, Licorice. Licorice adores the fish toy Coconut gives her, and Coconut can't wait to play with her bone-shaped toy.

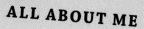

Sailor-style hat

Inflatable beach ring

Fun in the sun

Coconut loves a day at the beach. Her favorite activities include playing in the waves with her floaty, digging in the sand, and playing fetch with her lobster chew toy.

ALL ABOUT ME

★ **Personality:** Cuddly, loyal, adventurous

★ **Favorite activities:** Hiding slippers and chasing balls

★ **Best hangouts:** Her bed, the beach, and by her favorite girl's side

CHOCOLATE CHIP

Named for his breed, Chocolate Chip is a chocolate Labrador retriever, sometimes called a "chocolate lab." He's as sweet as they come and is always a loyal and trustworthy friend. Chocolate Chip is full of puppy energy and will happily play fetch with just about anything.

Soft tail

ALL ABOUT ME

★ Personality: **Energetic, friendly, gentle**

★ Favorite activities: **Swimming and jumping in puddles**

★ Best hangouts: **At the swimming pool and by the lake**

Sweet dreams

Whether catching a quick nap or settling in for a night of dream-filled slumber, Chocolate Chip loves to snuggle up in his comfy pet bed.

Chocolate Chip

Bright dog tag

GINGER

Ginger is the *purr*-fect kitty companion. True to her name, Ginger has a zingy personality—she is filled with playful pluck and is always up for fun. When she's had her fill of frisky frolicking, Ginger's sweet side shines through as she snuggles in for a nap.

DID YOU KNOW?
Calico cats like Ginger are not actually a breed but instead a color pattern of different-sized patches.

Cat napping

Ginger loves a big bed for catching up on lazy-day catnaps. At night, she curls up at the foot of the bed for sweet dreams near her favorite girl.

Purple collar

ALL ABOUT ME

★ Personality: **Playful, loving, and very creative**

★ Favorite activities: **Chase the toy mouse, hide-and-seek**

★ Best nap spot: **Sunny windowsills**

HONEY

Honey, an active golden retriever pup, loves to play, explore, and learn new tricks. Honey enjoys getting groomed and showing off her shiny coat, but that doesn't stop her from taking a swim when the water's just right.

ALL ABOUT ME

★ Personality: **Playful, cheerful, sporty**

★ Favorite activities: **Fetch, backyard obstacle course, and swimming**

★ Favorite nap spot: **Beneath a shady tree on a sunny day**

Puppy pedicure

Even a pup loves a little pampering time. When it's time for a spa day, Honey is sure to join in on the relaxing good time.

Fluffy golden fur

DID YOU KNOW?

Golden retrievers are eager to learn and easy to train. Many dog movies have a golden retriever as their star!

LICORICE

With shiny black-and-white fur and bright green eyes, Licorice is one pretty kitty. To get this American longhair's attention, just show her something sparkly. Licorice's rhinestone collar is her signature piece of jewelry, and she just adores playing dress-up.

DID YOU KNOW?

Even though the old saying goes "fight like cats and dogs," Licorice's very best friend is Coconut the pup.

ALL ABOUT ME

★ Personality: **Sweet, curious, and very glamorous**

★ Favorite activities: **Playing dress-up, especially with anything sparkly!**

★ Favorite hiding spot: **Paper bags**

Licorice

No scaredy cat

Some black cats might be a fright on Halloween, but Licorice is all sweetness. After all, the day is devoted to wearing cute costumes!

White patch at front

MEATLOAF

Meatloaf the bulldog is the cuddliest puppy around. His favorite pastime is snoozing, but when he's awake, he's set for fun—especially if treats are involved. Even though he's short in energy—and legs—Meatloaf makes up for it with a great big heart.

DID YOU KNOW?
When Meatloaf goes swimming, he needs a life vest. Like many in his breed, Meatloaf is too top-heavy to stay afloat with ease.

Canine concert
Meatloaf makes the perfect piano partner, even though he can't play a single note. Just tickle the ivories and he'll bark along to the tune.

ALL ABOUT ME

★ Personality: **Goofy, loveable, and laid-back**

★ Favorite activities: **Finding hidden treats and chewing on big bones**

★ Best hangouts: **Anywhere that's a good place for a nap**

Wrinkly paws

PEPPER

For Pepper the husky, the more snow there is, the better! His fur coat keeps him toasty warm when sliding across frozen ponds, dodging tossed snowballs, or—his very favorite—pulling a dog sled. He's full of energy and always ready to have *brrr*-illiant good times outside.

DID YOU KNOW?
When huskies like Pepper sleep in the cold, they cover their faces with their tails. This allows their warm breath to keep out the chill.

ALL ABOUT ME

★ Personality: **Peppy, bouncy, and full of life**

★ Favorite winter activity: **Sledding and catching snowflakes**

★ Favorite hangout: **On a stack of folded quilts**

Midnight blue name tag

Frosty fun
Climb aboard the winter sled for a chilly ride! Pepper is ready to head off on a snowy adventure.

PRALINE

When Praline, the gray tabby cat, isn't playing with toys and exploring the world around her, she loves to cuddle up on a warm lap. She's known for being clever, comforting, and very affectionate.

DID YOU KNOW?
The word "tabby" refers to a cat's striped or patterned coat. It is said to come from "atabi," a type of striped silk spun in Bangladesh.

ALL ABOUT ME

★ Personality: **Gentle, considerate, and peaceful**

★ Favorite activities: **Chasing balls of yarn and playing peek-a-boo**

★ Favorite hangout: **Curled up on a fluffy floor cushion**

Light blue eyes

Striped tabby pattern

Scrub-a-dub
Many cats don't like water, but Praline tolerates pampering in her paw-print pet bath. Her rubber ducky keeps her company as soaks up the suds.

SUGAR

Sugar may be itty-bitty in size, but she delivers serious style for such a small pooch. The tan, black, and white Yorkshire terrier, called a "Yorkie," has long hair that can be worn in lots of different ways. She loves everything to do with fashion, and dress-up is one of her favorite rainy day activities.

ALL ABOUT ME

★ Personality: **Sweet and smart**
★ Favorite activities: **Snuggling**
★ Best nap spot: **A great big pile of puffy pillows**

Raining cats and dogs

Too much time is devoted to styling Sugar's hair for it to get ruined in the rain. When wet weather is on its way, she takes cover beneath an adorable pet umbrella and slick raincoat.

Hair bow

Sugar

DID YOU KNOW?

While most dogs have fur, Yorkies have hair. If not trimmed regularly, their manes can grow up to two feet long.

Neatly trimmed hair

TOASTY

ALL ABOUT ME

★ Personality: **Smart, protective, playful**

★ Breed: **Collie**

★ Favorite activities: **Running obstacle courses and playing tag**

★ Favorite place: **The park**

Don't let Toasty's long fur coat make you believe she's just a pretty show dog seeking attention. While she won't turn down a good grooming session to keep her mane soft, she's a devoted dog who's more interested in protecting others than walking the doggie runways.

Fluffy tail

Toasty

Travel in style

Toasty's pet carrier means she can always travel in style. Surrounded by creature comforts of a treat bowl and paw-print blanket, Toasty feels right at home, even on the go.

DID YOU KNOW?
Collies like Toasty are sometimes used on farms to guard sheep. They make great pets, too!

SERVICE DOG

DID YOU KNOW?
Service dogs are trained to help with all kinds of different tasks, such as acting as a guide or carrying medical equipment.

This sweet service dog's single goal is to help others. He guides those who can't see or need help with balance when walking. If someone is scared, he's by her side to calm her. He receives praise for a job well done, but the smiling faces are reward enough.

Sturdy handle

Dog Log

SERVICE DOG IN TRAINING

Happy helper
While other dogs like to run through fields and play fetch, the service dog would rather be serving someone who needs help.

ALL ABOUT ME

★ Personality: **Loyal, helpful, generous**

★ Favorite activities: **Serving others in need**

★ Best nap spot: **In the grass beneath a shady tree**

Chapter 3
Perfect pastimes

Playing sports, creating art, dancing, or making music aren't just for fun. These hobbies also allow Truly Me™ girls to explore the world and discover who they really are.

BALLET

Budding ballerinas ready to take center stage put in plenty of practice before their big performance. In a dance filled with pirouettes, pliés, jumps, and spins, these girls are sure to steal the show as they leap into their starring roles.

Cropped sweater

Pink satin skirt

Black leotard

Top Tips

BALLET BASICS
1. Stand up tall for perfect posture.
2. Let the music be your guide.
3. No matter what, always have fun!

Puppy tutu

Tutu time
After a lot of practice time at the ballet barre, these girls are ready to dress the part and put on a ballet performance worthy of a standing ovation.

Lace-up ballet slippers

TAP DANCING

TOP TIPS

MAKE SOME NOISE

1. Relax your ankles for clean steps.
2. Lean forward for better balance when tapping.

Some choreography is about matching moves to music. With tap dancing, performers make music with their moves! Quick feet and a sense of rhythm help tap dancers perform their best. Outfits that shimmy and shake always add to the wow factor.

Glittery top hat

Make your move

From tap to jazz to ballet and more, today's girls know there's a dance style for anyone looking to move to the music.

Bow-tied tap shoes

129

BASKETBALL

Girls take it to the hoop with flair! Whether making a layup, going for three, or shooting a free throw, these girls give their all at every basketball game. Practicing is just as important as playing the big game, which is why these girls spend plenty of time on the court honing their skills.

★ American Girl

8

TOP TIPS

HOOP HELPERS

1. Bend your knees when shooting so that you start small and end tall.
2. Practice ball control by dribbling around cones.

★ American Girl

10

Team players

While each player brings a different skill to the team, the girls always work as one to score the most points and play their best.

Sport shorts

Yellow laces

TENNIS AND SOCCER

Playing a sport can mean kicking a ball on the field or swinging a racket on the court. Today's girls love to be active in fun ways they can enjoy with friends. They have a competitive spirit, but they know how to be good sports, too.

TOP TIPS

CHOOSING A NEW SPORT

1. Pick a sport that interests you.
2. Be patient—the more you practice, the easier it gets.

Striped tennis dress

Player number

Go team!

If you're a fan on the sidelines, cheering loud and proud shows team spirit and helps inspire the players to do their best.

SKIING AND SNOWBOARDING

When it's time to hit the slopes, girls bundle up in brightly patterned, eye-catching gear that's sure to look great against the white powdery snow. Whether they're swooshing on skis or sliding on snowboards, their outfits always include a helmet for safety in case they take a tumble.

TOP TIPS

SNOW BUNNY
1. The warmer you are, the more fun you'll have in the cold.
2. Start on the easy slopes and work your way up.

Purple ski jacket

Aqua helmet

Color-block boots

Jump on board
Girls who like surfing in the ocean or skating on the sidewalk are sure to love snowboarding down snowy slopes when winter temperatures turn chilly.

Ski poles

ICE-SKATING

Before performing to a crowd, these girls practice their skating skills. Gliding along on single blades requires good balance, but once they master that, it's all fun and games. As their skills improve, the girls put on impressive ice-skating shows to show off their twirling tricks and high-flying leaps.

Center ice

Skating in front of judges can be daunting, but girls do their best by staying relaxed and remembering to always have fun.

Silvery laces

TOP TIPS

SKATE SMART

1. Practice walking in skates on dry land first.
2. Place hands on bent knees to feel more stable.
3. Start with little steps on the ice.

133

ART

Aspiring artists set up their easels and enjoy creating their own mini-masterpieces. While their artwork may only hang on their bulletin boards for now, these girls dream of one day having their framed works on display in galleries and museums.

Art supplies

Artist's Toolbox

Colorful creativity

Creative girls use scraps of paper to create bright, bold patterns. These colorful works of modern art look great on walls or wrapped around gifts.

Painting smock

TOP TIPS

ART STARTS

1. Start with a sketch of your idea.
2. Paint what you know.
3. Look for inspiration all around you.

CRAFTS

TOP TIPS

CRAFTY KEEPSAKES

1. Turn items you'd normally throw away into recycled art.
2. Add your own touches to personalize greeting cards.
3. Print out pictures and make a scrapbook.

From colorful clothing and sparkly jewelry to great gifts for friends and family, crafting is the go-to hobby for girls wanting to add personal touches to everyday items. Each girl's one-of-a-kind style shines through when she embellishes items based on her own creative ideas.

Tee-rific trends

Fashion-forward girls love to stand out in a crowd. They use fabric paint and creative flair to turn basic tees into original styles.

Fabric paint

Brush cup

135

CAMPING

TOP TIPS

CAMPING ESSENTIALS

1. Sturdy tent
2. Sleeping bag
3. Flashlight

Sometimes it's fun to have a sleepover under the stars. Camping with friends is a great way to enjoy the sights and sounds of nature. Friends can share spooky stories, sing songs, and cook up delicious s'mores around a cozy campfire.

Zippered tent

Campfire

Hit the trail

There are so many things to do on a camping trip. Riding bikes on trails with a furry friend is another good way to explore the great outdoors.

Comfy shoes

GARDENING

Tending a vegetable patch or caring for beautiful flowers are great ways for budding gardeners to have fun in the sun. Gardening is also the perfect opportunity to spot wildlife, such as butterflies, beetles, and birds.

TOP TIPS

CARING FOR FLOWERS

1. Don't give a plant too much or too little water.
2. Make sure the plant gets plenty of sunlight.
3. Remove dead blossoms.

Garden tools

Gardeners can grow plants with seeds, a spade, and a watering can. A birdfeeder is great for attracting wildlife.

Beehive

Spade for digging

Gardening bench

Flowery collar

Watering can

HORSEBACK RIDING

Girls love to spend time with horses, and with so many equestrian activities to try, there's no shortage of fun. From trail-riding and showing to grooming and cleaning stalls, life around the stable is never boring.

Stable with swing gate

RISING STAR STABLES

TOP TIPS

STABLE SAFETY

1. Stay focused and calm in the presence of horses.
2. Never approach a horse from behind.
3. Riding horses should always be done with adult supervision.

Stable shovel

Soft chestnut foal

Giddyup

For sporty style when on the trails, a tucked-in shirt, stretchy pants, knee-high boots, and a helmet look great and keep riders safe, too.

Cowboy hat

Western show saddle

Show bridle

PIANO

For piano-loving girls, it feels extra-special to play on a grand piano. Whether it's a classical concert, a piano lesson, or simply some extra practice, girls are sure to create sweet music playing on such a beautiful instrument.

Carry a tune

To prepare for a spotlight recital in front of an audience, girls work hard and practice to stay relaxed and avoid stage fright.

Sheet music

Shiny black finish

Foot pedals

TOP TIPS

PIANO PERFECTION

1. Look over the sheet music before playing.
2. Play in front of friends and family to build confidence.
3. Keep hands warm before performing.

MUSIC GROUP

While solos are fun, musical girls enjoy playing together, too. Different instruments can be blended together to create a pop, rock, classical, folk, or country sound. Girls in music groups have to focus on playing their best while also working together.

TOP TIPS

MUSIC NOTES

1. Choose songs that everyone will enjoy.
2. Look for ways to put a twist on a well-known song.
3. Swap tips with each other.

Cello strings

Concert duo

Two instruments can be double the fun, especially when friends pair up to play beautiful duets together.

Pink knee socks

SLEEPOVER

Bedtime doesn't have to be a snore when friends stay the night for a fun-filled sleepover. A slumber party is the perfect time to share silly stories, watch favorite movies, dance to popular songs, share sweet snacks, and play fun board games.

Reversible pillow

TOP TIPS

PARTY PERFECTION

1. Pick a theme for games, food, and decorations.
2. Set up a space for friends to sleep before they arrive.
3. Plan lots of fun activities that everyone will enjoy.

Card game

Pajama top with ruffled hem

Sleeping bag

Sleep soundly

A two-in-one trundle bed is perfect for a slumber party. When girls get tired, the bed rolls out for a comfy night's sleep.

Flower-shaped throw pillow

Karaoke fun

Make sure the sleepover is a success with food, games, and entertainment. Everyone can sing along to their favorite tunes with a karaoke DVD.

Blossom bedding

Pet bed

BAKING

Whether whipping up a cake or a batch of cupcakes, there's nothing more fun than baking sweet treats to eat—for birthdays, parties, or just because! With a little bit of creativity, girls can create a whole range of tasty delights perfect for any occasion.

TOP TIPS

BETTER BAKING

1. Master the basics first.
2. Remember to measure all ingredients carefully.
3. Be creative when decorating your confections.

Cupcake stand

Tools of the trade

The right equipment can make the difference between a prize-winning cake or one that falls flat. Before baking, girls set up their stations with everything the recipe requires.

Oven mitt

COOKING

Girls love to stir up some fun in the kitchen, cooking delicious meals and tasty snacks to share with friends. With a kitchen stocked with all the right tools and appliances, budding chefs can't fail to impress with their culinary creations.

Hooks for hanging utensils

Pantry cupboard

TOP TIPS
TOP CHEF

1. Always taste your food before serving.
2. Follow a recipe once before trying to make a change.
3. Keep food simple when cooking for crowds.

Get cooking

Some girls have a sweet tooth while others may like savory snacks. Not everyone likes the same things, but it means more treats for all to try!

Chapter 4
Amazing places

Where do American Girl characters find inspiration? Anywhere! In a tree house in the backyard or a rainforest house in Brazil. Onstage, in the spotlight, or at home, in a cozy bedroom. No place is too big or too small.

KAYA'S TEPEE

Kaya and her family travel with the seasons to gather food, so their tepees are designed to be easily packed up and moved. Poles form the frame of the tepee and are covered with hides and tule mats. Inside, Kaya sleeps on a soft bedroll and furry pillow. When it's cold, she wraps up in warm furs and hides.

Tepee pole

Stepping outside

Kaya enjoys sleeping in her tepee, but she likes being outside best—that's where her horses are. She looks forward to greeting Steps High and Sparks Flying every morning.

Bed roll

Tule mat covering

FELICITY'S STABLES

Felicity loves visiting the stables to see Penny and her foal, Patriot. Felicity feeds and brushes the horses and cleans the stables with the help of her wheelbarrow. The horses are a lot of work, but Felicity loves spending time with them.

Penny

Patriot

Wheelbarrow with feed bags

Shovel

Cute and cozy
Felicity's friend Elizabeth often visits the stables. Together they help Patriot stay warm by dressing him in a cozy plaid coat.

149

CAROLINE'S PARLOR

Caroline often spends her winter afternoons sitting in the parlor with her needlework. From here, she can gaze out of the window at Lake Ontario and watch the ships coming and going. The fireplace means the room is always warm during the cold winter months.

DID YOU KNOW?
The parlor is where the Abbotts celebrate Christmas. The family gathers around the fireplace to exchange gifts.

Nautical painting

Lacy curtains

Storage drawers

Fire screen

A parlor party
During the War of 1812, Caroline is lucky that her family can still celebrate special occasions. They lay out their finest treats and table settings for the parties.

JOSEFINA'S WRITING DESK

Josefina's aunt brings this elegant desk all the way from Mexico City. Designed to be portable, it looks like a plain chest on the outside, but it's beautifully decorated on the inside. Josefina can store her notebook and writing supplies in the small drawers and compartments.

Decorated lid lifts up

Drawers to hold small items

Wooden stand

Remembering Mamá
Josefina can't wait until she can read the *cuaderno*, a leather notebook filled with her mother's favorite poems and sayings. This special notebook was created by Tía Dolores.

CÉCILE'S COURTYARD

Cécile spends summer days in the garden and courtyard of her New Orleans home. She plays tag with her young cousin and then rests in the hammock between the lemon trees. When Marie-Grace visits, Cécile lays out tasty treats for them on her pretty courtyard table.

Elaborate scrollwork

Matching table

Keeping cool
Cécile and Marie-Grace keep cool in the courtyard. For extra shade, Marie-Grace pops open her fashionable lace parasol.

KIRSTEN'S BED

Pioneer children rarely had their own bedrooms, but Kirsten has a cozy nook that's all her own. Her prettily painted wooden bed provides a soft place to play with Missy and her kittens, and her washstand has a little drawer that's perfect for storing her treasures.

DID YOU KNOW?
Early settlers didn't have closets in their cabins. Instead, they kept their clothes in wooden trunks.

Hair tied in neat braids

Warm and snug
Kirsten's cabin can get very cold on winter nights. Dressed in a full-length flannel nightgown and tucked under her warm quilt, Kirsten stays toasty and snug.

Kirsten's washstand

Warm stockings

SAMANTHA'S ICE CREAM PARLOR

Samantha is excited to visit Tyson's Ice Cream Parlor in New York City. Her aunt and uncle take her there as a special treat. There are so many delicious sweets to choose from, Samantha doesn't know how she will decide which one to have!

Cash register

Pretty in pink

From the pink countertops to the gleaming soda fountain, the parlor is as pretty as Samantha had imagined. She wears her favorite dress specially for the occasion.

Pretty ice cream bowls

Ornate chair

Soda glasses

Samantha's favorite ice cream flavor is peppermint.

Candy jar

TYSON'S
ICE CREAM
PARLOR

Ice cream containers

REBECCA'S MOVIE SET

Rebecca dreams of being an actress. Whether she's visiting a movie set with her cousin Max or dressing up and acting at home, she's happiest when she's performing. Rebecca's costume chest and collection of props are all she needs for inspiration.

Costume chest

Pages from a script

DIRECTOR

PRODUCTION TITLE:

SCENE: REEL #:

DIRECTOR:

DATE:

Butterfly Queen

In her school play, Rebecca flits gracefully across the stage in her role as the Butterfly Queen. Her brocade dress has a train in the back that unfolds into butterfly wings.

KIT'S TREE HOUSE

Kit's father builds her tree house using scraps of material. At first, Kit thinks it looks a bit plain, but she uses her imagination to spruce it up. Kit loves being in her tree house, writing stories for her newspaper or playing with her friend, Ruthie.

DID YOU KNOW?
Kit's friend Stirling helps her dad build the tree house as a surprise for Kit while she's busy babysitting!

Beaded chandelier

TREE HOUSE CLUB MEMBERS ONLY!

Going up
Grace the dog doesn't want to miss the fun, so Kit and Ruthie let her hitch a ride in the rope and bucket "elevator."

Rope and bucket "elevator"

MOLLY'S STAGE

Molly can't believe she has been chosen to perform as Miss Victory in her dance school's "Hooray for the U.S.A." show. The show is close to Molly's heart as it will raise money to help the war effort. Molly dances in the show while thinking of her father taking care of soldiers overseas.

Colored stage lights

Theater curtains

Movie time

Molly loves watching movies on the big screen. She chooses her favorite snack to eat while she waits for the film to start.

Pullout stairs

MARYELLEN'S SEASIDE DINER

Maryellen looks forward to going to the Seaside Diner with her friends after school. Sometimes she shares a booth with her sister, Joan, and Joan's boyfriend, Jerry. Maryellen especially loves the burgers and shakes. When the bell dings, their order is up!

DID YOU KNOW?
Maryellen's favorite seat is one of the counter stools. She likes to watch the cooks whip up the diners' meals.

Order slips for cook

Service bell

Counter stools

Striped apron

Padded corner booth

Rock and roll

At the jukebox, Maryellen can flip through songs, push a button to choose her favorite, and then pop in a nickel to hear it play.

MELODY'S STUDIO

DID YOU KNOW?
Melody comes up with the name for her brother's singing group, The Three Ravens.

When Melody's brother, Dwayne, gets the opportunity to record a song, he asks Melody to sing backup. Melody is thrilled to visit a real recording studio, but she is also a little nervous. With help from her brother, Melody overcomes her nerves and sings from the heart.

Music reels

Quiet Please...
RECORDING
IN PROGRESS

10:00
Session
Melody

Making music
In the recording booth, Melody puts on a pair of headphones so that she can hear the background music. She then sings her part into a microphone.

Adjustable music stand

Headphones

JULIE'S BEDROOM

DID YOU KNOW?
Julie's mom owns a shop called Gladrags that sells homemade items like jewelry, purses, lampshades, and rugs.

For Julie, moving to a new apartment with her mom and sister means a brand-new bedroom to decorate. Julie chooses a four-poster bed with brightly colored bedding and funky beaded curtains.

Purple four-poster bed

Beaded curtains

Floral bedspread

In her room
Julie loves spending time in the room that she helped decorate. Sitting in her egg chair, she can call her friends, listen to music, enjoy snacks, or just kick back and relax.

MARISOL'S STAGE

Marisol loves nothing more than dancing! When she moves to a new neighborhood with no dance studio, Marisol persuades a local dancer to begin teaching classes. Marisol won't let anything stand in the way of her dream to become a real dancer.

DID YOU KNOW?
Marisol is inspired to take ballet lessons when her mom takes her to see *The Nutcracker*.

In the spotlight
When Marisol has the opportunity to perform on stage, she jumps at the chance. In her rhinestone tiara and sparkly tutu, Marisol really shines.

Spinning stage

Pink spotlights

JESS'S TREE SWING

Palm tree

When Jess and her parents travel to Belize to study ancient Mayan ruins, Jess can't wait to hike, kayak, and explore. At the end of each day, she sits in her swinging chair, listens to the sounds of the jungle, and plans the next day's adventure.

Swinging chair

DID YOU KNOW?
Jess stays in Belize for five months. She's home-schooled so she doesn't fall behind with her studies.

Under the stars
At night, Jess curls up in her chair with her beloved stuffed monkey, Toshi. She writes in her journal or reads letters from her brother and sister back home.

Woven throw blanket

CHRISSA'S CRAFT STUDIO

Every crafty girl needs a place to get creative. When Chrissa comes to live with her grandmother, she creates a space for Chrissa to work. In the studio, Chrissa can sketch out her ideas and then bring them to life with yarn, needles, and thread.

DID YOU KNOW?
Chrissa's father made the bowl that holds her yarn and knitting needles.

Sketchbook for project ideas

Space for storing supplies

Craft chat

After a busy day at school, Chrissa likes to come home and work on her crafts with her grandmother. She finds it helps her to relax, and it's a good time to talk about any problems at school.

CHRISSA'S PICNIC TABLE

Chrissa's friends Sonali and Gwen love joining her after school for a picnic by the lake. The girls fill the table with plenty of delicious snacks and drinks and discuss their day at school. When the girls decide to take a stand against bullying, it's the perfect place to gather other friends from school, too.

Hanging lanterns

Table talkers

Chrissa puts out a box of table talkers—cards printed with inspirational sayings—to help get the conversation started.

Table talkers

Polka-dot glasses

Spinning pinwheels

LANIE'S HAMMOCK

While her family prefers staying indoors, Lanie satisfies her adventurous outdoor spirit in her own backyard. When she's not learning about wildlife, spotting local birds, or tending to the wildflower garden she planted, she hangs out in her hammock and writes in her nature journal.

Sunburst pattern

Hammock stand

Comfy sandals

Animal spotting

Lanie enjoys bird-watching and is always on the lookout for new species. She loves to spot wildlife on the ground, too, such as the red fox and gray squirrel.

KANANI'S SHAVE ICE STAND

Living on the Hawaiian island of Kaua'i, Kanani is always ready to spread the "aloha spirit" of welcome and friendship. She enjoys meeting people and looks forwards to summer when she can help out at her family's shave ice stand.

Straw roof

PICK UP HERE

ORDER HERE

Shave ice machine

ALOHA

Aloha
Hawaii

Hawaiian
SHAVE ICE

Save the seals
While at the beach, Kanani spots a baby monk seal trapped in a net and helps rescue it. To help save the local monk seals, Kanani raises money and public awareness at the shave ice stand.

SAVE THE
MONK
SEALS!

FLAVORS OF THE DAY
Mango ★ Mandarin Orange ★ Watermelon ★ Strawberry ★ Coconut
see our menu for more!

"Save the seals" poster

McKenna's Bar and Beam

McKenna has her sights set on winning an Olympic gold medal one day. She knows she can achieve her dream if she works hard and believes in herself. McKenna spends all the time she can at the gym, perfecting her flips on the practice bar and rehearsing her tricky balance-beam routine.

DID YOU KNOW?
McKenna is part of a gymnastics team called the Twisters. She and her teammates use the practice bar to warm up before taking part in competitions.

Finding balance

McKenna uses the low-to-ground balance beam to learn new tricks. Giving her the confidence she needs, the practice beam helps McKenna perfect her moves before she tries them out on the higher beam.

Purple grips

Practice bar

☆ American Girl

Reversible gym mat

ISABELLE'S STUDIO

When she's not practicing her ballet routines, Isabelle designs custom dancewear using her sewing machine, dress form, and a stock of beautiful embellishments. She loves bringing her ideas to life and creating eye-catching looks. Isabelle's studio has everything she needs to fuel her creative spirit.

DID YOU KNOW?
While her sister inspires Isabelle to dance her best, her mom—whose career is restoring antique textiles—inspires Isabelle's flair for fashion.

Storage pockets

Inspirational fashion designs

Dress form

Sketch Book

★American Girl DRESS FORM

Upholstered stool

Two-for-one space
The other side of Isabelle's studio features two mirrors and a ballet barre. Isabelle goes through positions at the barre and works on perfecting her dance routines.

GRACE'S BAKERY

Grace is delighted to visit her aunt and uncle's French bakery, called a *pâtisserie*, in Paris for the summer. Grace feels lucky to learn how to bake French pastries, cakes, and tarts in a professional bakery with state-of-the-art baking equipment.

French bakery sign

La Pâtisserie

Le Menu
Our delicious French
pastries and breads

Pâtisseries

Les macarons
Sweet meringue filled with creamy ganache

Mille-feuilles aux fraises
Strawberry-layered puff pastry with
vanilla flavored cream

Plaisir sucré
Chocolate short layers with chocolate cream
topped with a toasted hazelnut

Tarte au citron vert
Lime tart with marshmallow cream topping

Tarte au chocolat
Rich chocolate tart topped with a raspberry

Tarte aux framboises
Raspberry-filled natural tart

Pain au chocolat
Hand-rolled, flaky chocolate-filled croissant

Pains

Baguette parisienne
Long white loaf bread with a crispy crust

Pain aux olives
Long white loaf bread with olives

Chalkboard menu

Take out boxes

Display shelf

On-the-go

Customers can eat their baked goods at the *pâtisserie*, or take them home to enjoy. Grace takes orders through the special window and serves up sweet treats to go.

DID YOU KNOW?
Grace takes inspiration from her aunt and uncle's Parisian bakery to set up her own pastry cart back home in Massachusetts.

Arched windows

Parisian treats

Monogrammed apron

Sidewalk café table

LEA'S RAINFOREST HOUSE

When Lea stays with her brother's host family deep in the Amazon jungle, she discovers the wonders of the Brazilian rainforest right outside her door. Lea is ready for a world of new sights and experiences—and she is ready to capture them all with her camera.

Jungle dwellers

Lea's favorite part of staying in the Amazon is seeing exotic animals. She spots many colorful butterflies and birds. On a hike through the rainforest, she finds an injured baby sloth.

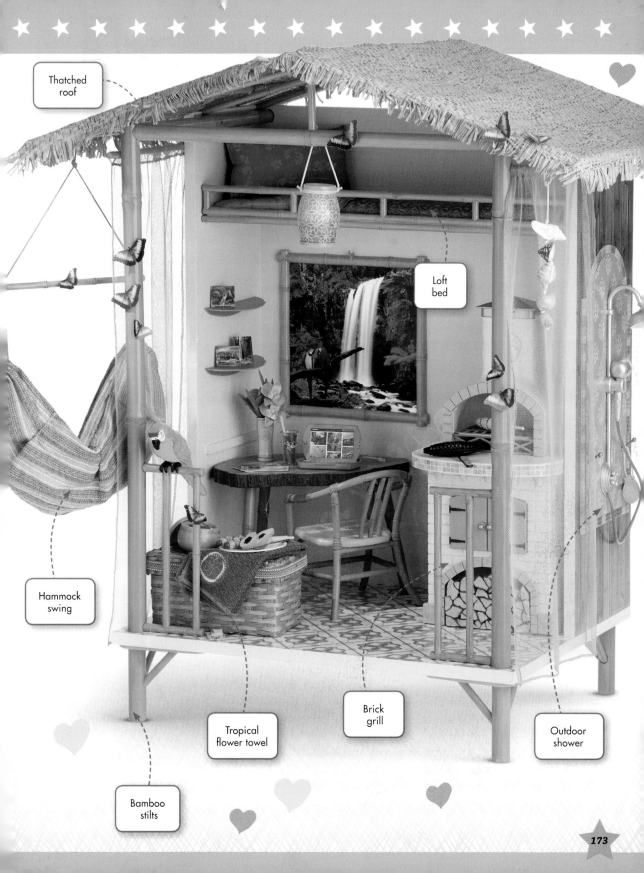

Thatched roof

Loft bed

Hammock swing

Tropical flower towel

Brick grill

Outdoor shower

Bamboo stilts

GABRIELA'S STUDIO

Gabriela loves to dance onstage, so she can't wait to perform her spoken-word poetry for an audience. Practicing in front of her poetry group in the studio gives Gabriela the confidence she needs to perform.

LISTEN TO YOUR ART

Practice mirror

In the studio
After dance practice, Gabriela takes some time to relax in the studio. She likes to listen to music to inspire her poetry.

Dance barre

Embroidered towel

American Girl
DANCE STUDIO
STUDIO HOURS:
MONDAY–SATURDAY
10 AM–9 PM

Z'S BEDROOM

Z is always on the lookout for a good story. She takes her camera wherever she goes, but her most creative work takes place in her bedroom. That's where she edits her footage into mini-movies.

Director's clapperboard

Light for filming

DID YOU KNOW?
Z makes stop-motion movies featuring American Girl dolls! In her vlog she gives tips on shooting stop-motion video.

Laptop for editing

Time to edit
At her laptop, Z watches back her footage, chooses the best clips, and adds music and sounds to complete her film. Then she shares it with her family and friends.

TENNEY'S DRESSING ROOM

Before a show, Tenney gets ready in the dressing room backstage. After she's put on her best outfit and eaten a snack for energy, Tenney shines under the bright lights of the stage while she sings and plays her six-string guitar.

Mirror with lights

ON AIR

LOVE DANCE SING

MUSIC

Good luck, Tenney!

Nashville

ROCK 'N' ROLL

Satin robe

Pre-show snacks

Tenney's tambourine

Tenney's
backdrop

Stage
light

Amplifier
for Tenney's
guitar

Microphone
stand

Pre-show nerves

Although Tenney loves
writing music and playing
her songs, she still gets
nervous before a show.
When she steps onstage,
she takes a deep breath
and imagines the people
in the audience all
wearing funny glasses!

Chapter 5
Girls on the go

How do girls explore their world? On bikes and in hot-air balloons. Paddling kayaks and cruising in convertibles. Wherever girls go, they make sure to enjoy the ride!

FELICITY'S CARRIAGE

When Felicity is invited to the Governor's Palace for a dancing lesson, she dresses in her finest gown. For such a special occasion, Felicity travels in a beautiful horse-drawn carriage. With soft tie-back curtains and lanterns to light the way, Felicity feels like a princess.

DID YOU KNOW?
Felicity's quilted bench seat lifts up to reveal a hidden storage compartment underneath. Felicity can keep secret treasures in her carriage.

A magical view
Felicity admires the snow-covered landscape as she travels to the Governor's Palace. It's a magical ride.

Fabric roof

Lanterns

Bridle and reins

Velvety curtains

Carriage poles

CAROLINE'S SKIFF

One of Caroline's favorite things to do is go sailing with her papa on Lake Ontario, especially in her very own boat. Papa repaired this wooden skiff and named it *Miss Caroline*. When Caroline sits inside and reaches for the oars, she feels right at home.

Into the sunset

During the day, Caroline shades her eyes with a wide-brimmed hat. When the sun sets over the lake, she takes off her hat and takes in the beautiful view.

DID YOU KNOW?
Caroline's papa built the two-seater boat himself at the family's shipyard.

Mast with canvas sail

Wooden oar

Painted name "Miss Caroline"

SAMANTHA'S BICYCLE

Uncle Gard gives Samantha a pretty pink bicycle and teaches her how to ride it in Grandmary's driveway. To make riding easier, Samantha wears checkered bloomers instead of a skirt and black gaiters to cover her legs and keep her shoes clean. With her sun hat on, Samantha is ready to roll off on an adventure.

DID YOU KNOW?
On her first day of riding, Samantha swerves off the path and splashes into the lake! But she finds the courage to try again.

Woven basket

Bloomers

In the park
Once she gets the hang of riding, Samantha takes her bicycle to the park. Her dog, Jip, loves to run along beside her.

Gaiters

SAMANTHA AND NELLIE'S SLEIGH

One Christmas morning, Samantha and Nellie ride in a horse-drawn sleigh. The girls feel like they are in a magical winter wonderland as they glide over the snow with jingle bells ringing. It's chilly outside, but Samantha and Nellie keep warm under a cozy flannel blanket.

Holiday garland

Reins

DID YOU KNOW?
Nellie and Samantha glide through Central Park in New York City when they take their very first sleigh ride.

Jingle bells

Winter finery
Samantha and Nellie bundle up in beautiful new coats for their holiday sleigh ride. Their outfits are warm, stylish, and festive, too.

JULIE'S CAR

When Julie hears that bald eagles are endangered, she wants to help save them. She holds a charity car wash with her best friend, Ivy. The money they raise goes to help save bald eagles. They work hard to make this brand-new blue 1974 Volkswagen Super Beetle convertible clean and shiny.

DID YOU KNOW?
The car's license plate reads "SFGIRL." The "SF" stands for San Francisco—Julie's home city in California.

At the car wash

Equipped with a bucket, soap, window washer, and cloths, Julie and Ivy make cars gleam for a good cause. It's hard work, but the girls know that saving the bald eagle is worth it.

Lowered canvas top

Sky blue paint

White interior seating

Rolling wheels

JULIE'S BICYCLE

In 1976, Julie's neighborhood celebrates the United States Bicentennial, which marks 200 years since America declared that it would no longer be ruled by Great Britain. Decked out in red, white, and blue with patriotic stars on the wheels, Julie's banana-seat bike is the star of her neighborhood parade.

DID YOU KNOW?

Julie sometimes brings her pet rabbit, Nutmeg, along for the ride. He sits in the basket as Julie gently rolls through the neighborhood.

Handlebar streamers

Fun on wheels

Julie gets a workout biking up and down the hilly streets of San Francisco. With her best friend by her side, Julie has fun, even on the steep hills!

Star wheel decorations

Balancing kickstand

LANIE'S CAMPER

DID YOU KNOW?
When weather doesn't allow Lanie to sleep under the stars, she can pull down the message board in the camper to create a bed.

With her best friend far away in Indonesia working with baby orangutans, Lanie feels bored staying at home for the summer. When her aunt Hannah visits in her camper, Lanie jumps at the chance to go on an outdoor adventure.

Message board

Storage bench

Door with window

Mini fridge

Tight spaces
Campers may look small, but they can fit a lot in a little space. Lanie's camper has a shower, mini fridge, stove, and even a hidden bed.

SAIGE'S HOT-AIR BALLOON

Saige feels lucky having a hot-air balloon pilot for a dad. It means she can soar into the sky above her home in Albuquerque, New Mexico. The amazing views inspire Saige's paintings. She also likes to take trips through the clouds with her grandmother Mimi.

American Girl

Envelope (balloon)

Wicker basket

Family fun
Saige prepares the basket before she and her dad take off into the picturesque New Mexican sky.

DID YOU KNOW?
Saige uses a map of Albuquerque and a pilot's logbook to help her dad track where they're flying and make notes about each of their flights.

Opening door

LEA'S KAYAK

Lea is ready to explore all that Brazil has to offer, from its lush rainforests to its tropical beaches. She can't wait to take her kayak out on the water to see the colorful fish that swim beneath the waves!

Kayaking gear

Lea brings plenty of supplies with her when she goes kayaking. She can keep her mask and snorkel, waterproof camera, and sunscreen in the storage area behind her seat.

Sail that swivels

DID YOU KNOW?
Lea's kayak has a clear bottom, so she can see underwater without having to dive in.

Clear bottom

Colorful paddle

Z'S SCOOTER

With so much to capture on film, aspiring filmmaker Z often feels like she needs to be in two places at once. On her trusty scooter, she can zip around town in no time at all. The three-wheeled design means that Z can step off to make videos wherever inspiration takes her.

DID YOU KNOW?
Z often brings her dog, Popcorn, on filming trips around town. Popcorn loves to run alongside Z's scooter.

Striped helmet

Knee pads

Moving images
Z's scooter isn't just great for getting around, it can be a moving tripod, too. Attaching a camera to the front means that Z never misses a second of the action.

Z's Dalmatian, Popcorn

PRETTY CITY CARRIAGE

In this elegant horse-drawn carriage, girls can ride in style atop a tufted velvety seat. A chestnut-brown horse guides them on a winter-white tour of the city while jingle bells add whimsical music to the journey.

DID YOU KNOW?
Perfect for seeing star-filled skies, the carriage canopy folds down, offering a beautiful view on a bright, twinkly night.

Folding canopy cover

Travel in style

Fit for a princess headed to the ball, this carriage delivers girls to their destinations with an added touch of glamour.

Silver foil trim

Jingle bells

TRAIL BIKE

With this special bike, a girl can hit the trail with her favorite furry friend tagging along. A girl's canine companion enjoys the views in a pet trailer that matches her pretty purple bike. Together, the duo ride off on adventures.

DID YOU KNOW?
This sporty cycling outfit includes a bright yellow jersey and yellow striped cycling shorts, so that the rider can stay safe by always being visible to others.

Mesh windows

Bike-rack bag

Pedal power
Exploring the great outdoors has never been easier with this bike built for hitting the trails. Everything a girl needs while riding fits neatly into her bike-rack bag.

MOTOR SCOOTER

See the sights in style on the back of a purple scooter that's sure to catch the eyes of others on the streets. Rev up for a great ride featuring a comfy cushioned seat, rearview mirrors, a speedometer, gas gauge, and a headlight. Exploring the neighborhood has never been so much fun.

DID YOU KNOW?
What makes a motor scooter different from a motorcycle is that it has a step-through frame and a platform for the rider's feet.

Super storage
Girls can store all their treasures in the silver basket before zooming off on an adventure with their best friends.

Mirror

Headlight

Double wheel for balance

192

CAMPING TRAILER

Get back to nature in this home-away-from-home pop-up camper. Girls camp in comfort with a cute kitchenette and a comfy fold-away bed that creates extra storage when not in use. Mealtimes are easy with a stove to cook warm meals that can be enjoyed with friends around the glow of a cozy campfire.

DID YOU KNOW?
Camping requires a lot of supplies, so storage is key. This pop-up trailer features plenty of places to tuck away everything needed to sleep outdoors.

Festive mini lights

Pop-up canopy

Decorative stickers

Luggage loading
When the camper is all packed up, the canopy frame doubles as a luggage rack. It makes for extra easy travel when out exploring the open road.

Character gallery

The American Girl characters dream big dreams and work hard to overcome challenges. Their stories inspire girls of today to do their best and never let anything stand in the way of what's important to them.

BEFOREVER COLLECTION

Kaya™
1764

Felicity Merriman™
1774

Elizabeth Cole™
1775

Caroline Abbott™
1812

Josefina Montoya™
1824

Cécile Ray™
1853

Marie-Grace Gardner™ 1853

Kirsten Larson™
1854

Addy Walker™
1864

Samantha Parkington™ 1904

Nellie O'Malley™
1906

Rebecca Rubin™
1914

Kit Kittredge™
1934

Ruthie Smithens™
1932

Molly McIntire™
1944

Emily Bennett
1944

Maryellen Larkin
1954

Melody Ellison
1964

Julie Albright
1974

Ivy Ling
1976

★ GIRL OF THE YEAR COLLECTION ★

Lindsey Bergman
2001

Kailey Hopkins
2003

Marisol Luna
2005

Jess McConnell
2006

Nicki Fleming
2007

Mia St. Clair
2008

Chrissa Maxwell
2009

Sonali Matthews
2009

Gwen Thompson
2009

Lanie Holland
2010

Kanani Akina
2011

McKenna Brooks
2012

Saige Copeland
2013

Isabelle Palmer
2014

Grace Thomas
2015

Lea Clark
2016

Gabriela McBride
2017

★ INTRODUCED IN 2017 ★

Tenney Grant
2017

Z Yang
2017

Truly Me™ gallery

Truly Me dolls encourage girls to really express themselves. With so many different looks to choose from, each girl can find a special companion to reflect her own unique style.

Long red hair, green eyes

Dark-brown hair, brown eyes

Light-brown hair, brown eyes

Dark-brown bangs, brown eyes

Blonde bangs, blue eyes

Brown curly hair, brown eyes

Light-brown bob, brown eyes

Long brown hair, brown eyes

Blonde curly hair, hazel eyes

Long black hair, blue eyes

Bobbed light-red hair, green eyes

Black bangs, brown eyes

Long blonde hair, blue eyes

Long curly brown hair, hazel eyes

Blonde bangs, green eyes

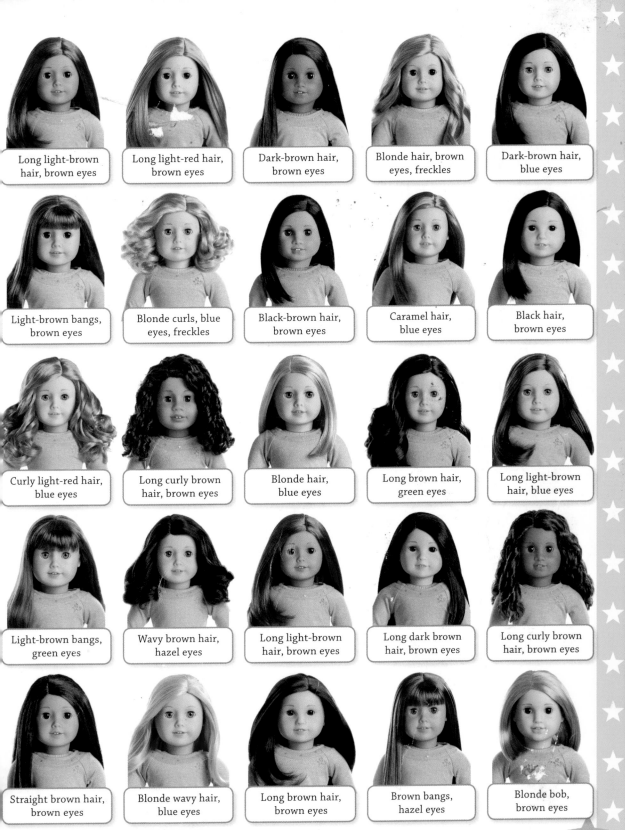

Long light-brown hair, brown eyes

Long light-red hair, brown eyes

Dark-brown hair, brown eyes

Blonde hair, brown eyes, freckles

Dark-brown hair, blue eyes

Light-brown bangs, brown eyes

Blonde curls, blue eyes, freckles

Black-brown hair, brown eyes

Caramel hair, blue eyes

Black hair, brown eyes

Curly light-red hair, blue eyes

Long curly brown hair, brown eyes

Blonde hair, blue eyes

Long brown hair, green eyes

Long light-brown hair, blue eyes

Light-brown bangs, green eyes

Wavy brown hair, hazel eyes

Long light-brown hair, brown eyes

Long dark brown hair, brown eyes

Long curly brown hair, brown eyes

Straight brown hair, brown eyes

Blonde wavy hair, blue eyes

Long brown hair, brown eyes

Brown bangs, hazel eyes

Blonde bob, brown eyes

Animal gallery

Animal friends come in all shapes and sizes. They can be furry, fuzzy, or even feathered. Pets make the perfect sidekicks, adding fun playtime and cozy cuddles whenever needed.

Kaya's Appaloosa, Steps High

Felicity's horse, Penny

Caroline's cat, Inkpot

Josefina's goat, Sombrita

Cécile's parrot, Cochon

Marie-Grace's dog, Argos

Kirsten's gray cat, Missy

Addy's canary, Sunny

Samantha's cocker spaniel, Jip

Rebecca's rescue kittens

Kit's basset hound, Grace

Molly's terrier puppy, Bennett

Emily's terrier puppy, Yank

Maryellen's dachshund, Scooter

Melody's puppy, Bo

Julie's bunny, Nutmeg

Kailey's golden retriever, Sandy

Marisol's cat, Rascal

Nicki's dog, Sprocket

Nicki's buckskin horse, Jackson

Chrissa's llama, Starburst

Lanie's rabbit, Lulu

Lanie's woodland creatures

Kanani's dog, Barksee

McKenna's puppy, Cooper

Saige's horse, Picasso

Saige's Border Collie, Sam

Isabelle's white cat, Tutu

Grace's French Bulldog, Bonbon

West Highland Terrier, Coconut

Labrador puppy, Chocolate Chip

Calico cat, Ginger

Retriever puppy, Honey

American Longhair cat, Licorice

Bulldog puppy, Meatloaf

Husky puppy, Pepper

Tabby cat, Praline

Yorkshire Terrier, Sugar

Collie, Toasty

Service Dog

BeForever™ accessories

Every BeForever character comes with her own range of historically accurate accessories. Through these accessories, girls of today can really explore what life was like in the past.

Kaya's drum and mallet

Kaya's fringed saddle

Felicity's tea chair

Felicity's fashion doll

Felicity's Noah's Ark toy

Elizabeth's fancy fan

Caroline's winter cap

Caroline's ice skates

Josefina's embroidered gold shawl

Josefina's weaving loom

Cécile's glass fruit-bowl

Cécile's ribbon-and-floral mask

Marie-Grace's lacy parasol

Marie-Grace's vanity set

Kirsten's painted trunk

Kirsten's patchwork quilt

Addy's bean doll, Ida

Addy's straw bonnet

Samantha's basket of tulips

Samantha's tea set

Nellie's Celtic cross necklace

Nellie's drawstring bag

Rebecca's dominoes

Rebecca's phonograph

Kit's strawberry-print apron

Kit's camera case

Ruthie's slippers

Molly's movie popcorn

Molly's Miss Victory costume

Molly's khaki sleeping bag

Emily's wooden sled

Emily's ration book

Maryellen's poodle skirt

Maryellen's TV set

Melody's radio

Melody's purse

Julie's skateboard

Julie's knee-high boots

Ivy's chocolate fondue set

Ivy's purple beret

Girl of the Year™ accessories

Whether it's dancing, painting, sports or baking, every GOTY has her own favorite hobby—and a whole host of exciting accessories to go with it!

Lindsey's notebook and pen

Lindsey's laptop computer

Kailey's stand-up paddle board

Kailey's tide pool guide book

Marisol's purple ballet slippers

Marisol's glittery rhinestone tiara

Jess's butterfly-shaped camera

Jess's tropical tankini

Nicki's tack box

Nicki's western-style hat

Nicki's snow goggles

Mia's walrus stuffed animal

Mia's accessory storage case

Chrissa's three-tiered cake

Chrissa's polka-dot picnic cups

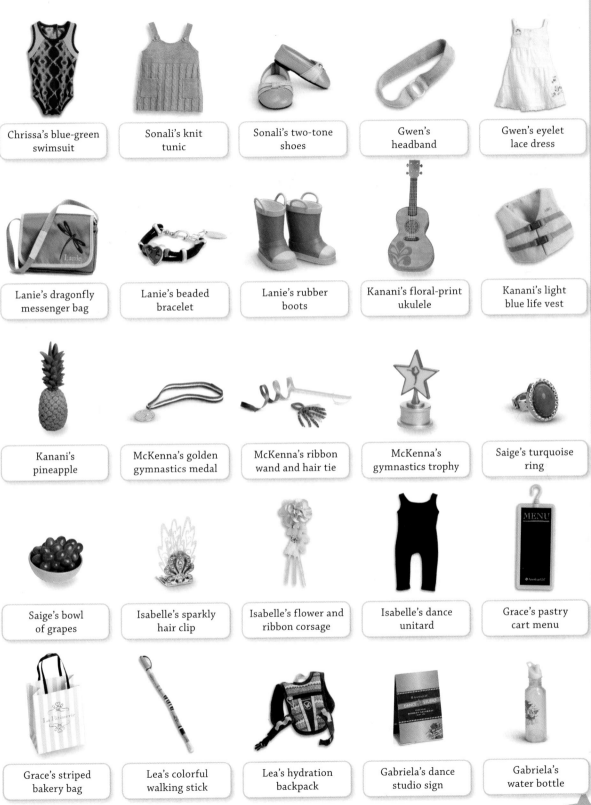

Chrissa's blue-green swimsuit

Sonali's knit tunic

Sonali's two-tone shoes

Gwen's headband

Gwen's eyelet lace dress

Lanie's dragonfly messenger bag

Lanie's beaded bracelet

Lanie's rubber boots

Kanani's floral-print ukulele

Kanani's light blue life vest

Kanani's pineapple

McKenna's golden gymnastics medal

McKenna's ribbon wand and hair tie

McKenna's gymnastics trophy

Saige's turquoise ring

Saige's bowl of grapes

Isabelle's sparkly hair clip

Isabelle's flower and ribbon corsage

Isabelle's dance unitard

Grace's pastry cart menu

Grace's striped bakery bag

Lea's colorful walking stick

Lea's hydration backpack

Gabriela's dance studio sign

Gabriela's water bottle

Truly Me™ accessories

Accessories are a small way to make a big statement! From sports equipment to fancy jewelry, school supplies to holiday gear, these extra details help bring a doll's character to life.

Acoustic guitar and music books

Set of two crutches

Artist's easel and paints

Back-to-school backpack

White and blue western hat

TV with DVDs and remote control

White and blue doll-size Heelys®

Bowling pins and bowling ball

Box of luxury chocolates

Silver menorah

Blue purse with flower detail

Soccer trophy

Blue skateboard with star pattern

Funky beach sunglasses

Colorful pencil case

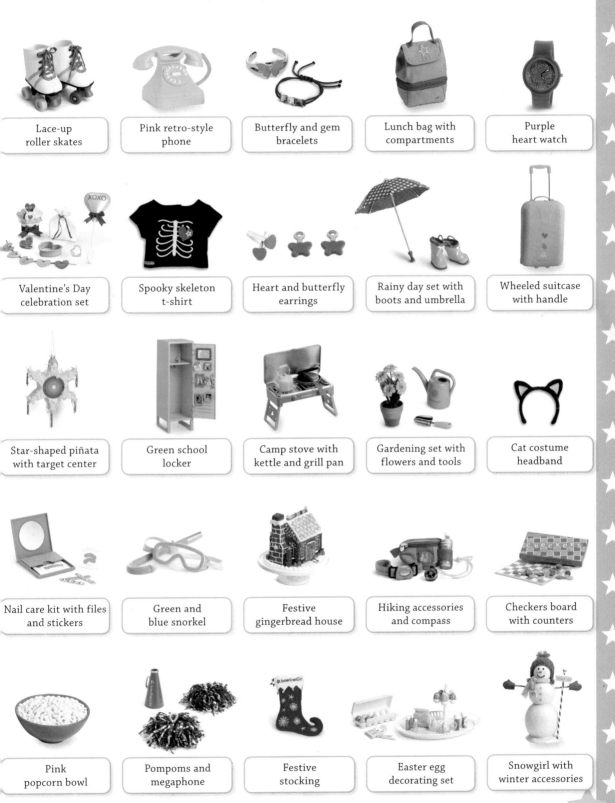

Lace-up
roller skates

Pink retro-style
phone

Butterfly and gem
bracelets

Lunch bag with
compartments

Purple
heart watch

Valentine's Day
celebration set

Spooky skeleton
t-shirt

Heart and butterfly
earrings

Rainy day set with
boots and umbrella

Wheeled suitcase
with handle

Star-shaped piñata
with target center

Green school
locker

Camp stove with
kettle and grill pan

Gardening set with
flowers and tools

Cat costume
headband

Nail care kit with files
and stickers

Green and
blue snorkel

Festive
gingerbread house

Hiking accessories
and compass

Checkers board
with counters

Pink
popcorn bowl

Pompoms and
megaphone

Festive
stocking

Easter egg
decorating set

Snowgirl with
winter accessories

Index

Page numbers in **bold** refer to main entries.

Acknowledgments

Senior Editor Laura Palosuo
Senior Designer Lisa Sodeau
Pre-production Producer Kavita Varma
Senior Producer Louise Daly
Managing Editor Paula Regan
Design Manager Jo Connor
Publisher Julie Ferris
Art Director Lisa Lanzarini
Publishing Director Simon Beecroft

First American Edition, 2017
Published in the United States by DK Publishing
345 Hudson Street, New York, NY 10014

Page design copyright © 2017 Dorling Kindersley Limited

DK, a division of Penguin Random House LLC

17 18 19 20 21 10 9 8 7 6 5 4 3 2

002–299177–Jul/17

A catalog record for this book is available
from the Library of Congress.

ISBN: 978-1-4654-6079-0

DK books are available at special discounts when
purchased in bulk for sales promotions, premiums,
fund-raising, or educational use. For details,
contact: DK Publishing Special Markets,
345 Hudson Street, New York, NY 10014
SpecialSales@dk.com

Printed and bound in the USA

A WORLD OF IDEAS:
SEE ALL THERE IS TO KNOW

www.americangirl.com
www.dk.com

DK would like to thank Sara Hereley, Jennifer Hirsch,
Nancy Price, and Riley Wilkinson at American Girl
and Charnita Belcher at Mattel.

DK would also like to thank Tori Kosara and Eleanor
Rose for editorial help; Gema Salamanca for design
assistance; Joanne Rueloz Diaz for proofreading; and
Helen Peters for creating the index.